# About Quick & Healthy....

"At last. Practical tips for controlling fat and cholesterol, along with quick, healthy recipes that taste great. Highly recommended."

—John P. Foreyt, PhD, Director, Nutrition Research Clinic, Houston, Texas

*Quick & Healthy* is just what everyone is looking for — wonderful sounding recipes that can be prepared in minutes! Not only are the recipes appealing, the book is rich in imaginative and creative tips for "quick and healthy" shopping, cooking, and menu ideas..."

—Marion J. Franz, RD, MS, CDE, Vice President, Nutrition and Publications, International Diabetes Center, Minneapolis, Minnesota

"Brenda Ponichtera's book does an excellent job of helping even the non-cooks among us. This practical 'how to' guide includes menus, ideas for no-cook meals, weight control suggestions, food products worth selecting... and even the shopping list! I recommend that you take the time to buy this book..."

—Nancy Clark, MS, RD, Sports Nutritionist and author of *The Athlete's Kitchen* and *Nancy Clark's Sports Nutrition Guidebook*

"Just what people are looking for—a user friendly book about a lower fat, higher complex carbohydrate eating style. I particularly like the tips on reducing fat and cholesterol, the list of products worth trying, and the grocery lists..."

—Sonja L. Conner, MS, RD, Research Associate Professor, Oregon Health Sciences University and co-author of *The New American Diet* and *The New American Diet System*

"*Quick & Healthy* is not just another cookbook. The Time Saving Ideas, Quick Meals and Snacks, and Grocerys Lists make the book more like a kitchen almanac... Better yet are the quick, tasty and nutritious recipes. *Quick & Healthy* is a winner! A must-have for today's busy cooks!"

— Peggy Paul, RD, LD, Director, Oregon Dairy Council

# Quick

# & Healthy

## RECIPES AND IDEAS

*For people who say they don't have
time to cook healthy meals*

Brenda J. Ponichtera
Registered Dietitian

Library of Congress Catalog Card Number 91-90207

Publisher's Cataloging in Publication

Ponichtera, Brenda J.

   Quick and healthy recipes and ideas: for people who say they
don't have time to cook healthy meals / Brenda J. Ponichtera.
   p. cm.
   Includes index.
   ISBN 0-9629160-0-5

   1. Quick and easy cookery. 2. Low-fat diet—Recipes. 3. Low- cholesterol diet—Recipes.
4. Diabetes—Diet therapy—Recipes.
I. Title.
RM237.7                   641.5638
                   QBI91-1572


Typesetting: Great River Graphics, Lone Wolfe graphics & design
Cover & Design: Lisa Drake
Art Work: Janice Staver
Editing: Mary Schlick

Printed in the United States of America
1   2   3   4   5   6   7   8   9   10

Published by:
ScaleDown
—Brenda J. Ponichtera, R.D.
1519 Hermits Way
The Dalles, Oregon 97058

# ACKNOWLEDGEMENTS

My sincere appreciation to the following who contributed to this book:

Lisa Drake, graphic artist, who not only designed the cover, but set the design throughout the book.

Janice Staver, one of my favorite local artists, for her expert advice on color and for her wonderful artwork.

Claudia Schon, home economist and excellent cook, who searched out and tested recipes. Her family, Dick, Pat, and Jim, who sampled recipes.

Cathy Coreson-Carter, who tested recipes and offered many time-saving tips. Her husband, Ralph, who sampled and proofread recipes.

Sandy Anderson, who tested recipes and did the computer entry.


A special thank you to all of my patients and friends who gave support, ideas, and/or shared some of their favorite recipes.

And last, but not at all least, my husband, Ken, and children, Kevin and Kyle, for their support, patience, and willingness (most of the time!) to sample recipes.

*To Ken, Kevin, and Kyle*
*for supporting me in my work and for providing encouragement.*

# TABLE OF CONTENTS

# INTRODUCTION

Too often I see clients who say "I don't have the time to plan and cook healthy meals." It does take time to search out quick and healthy recipes that the entire family will enjoy. With that in mind, I decided to write this book.

I looked at the needs of my patients when planning what I should include. Those wanting to lose weight, those with elevated cholesterol, and those with diabetes. Most wanted recipes and ideas for quick meals that would help them reach their goals. They also wanted recipes that their whole family would enjoy.

*Quick & Healthy* is a compilation of kitchen and family tested recipes that can be put together in a short period of time. A few may take longer to cook but they do not require a lot of attention. Grocery lists for staples and perishables are also included. Make copies of the lists and keep them handy in the kitchen for checking what you need on your next grocery trip.

All of the recipes in *Quick & Healthy* are designed to be low in fat and cholesterol. Minimal amounts of oil and margarine are used and sodium is limited. Exchanges are listed for each recipe.

Please note that ingredients listed as optional are not included in the Nutrient Analysis of Recipes which is at the end of the book. If a choice of ingredients is given, the first is used in the Nutrient Analysis of Recipes.

Microwave directions are for a 700-watt microwave. Times will vary with different wattages.

Be sure to refer to the sections on Time Saving Ideas, Products Worth Trying, and Ideas for Quick Meals and Snacks. These three sections will give you more ways to save time without compromising good nutrition.

May this book help you in your search for quick and healthy meals.

Brenda J. Ponichtera
Registered Dietitian

# CHOLESTEROL-SATURATED FAT INDEX

The Nutrient Analysis of Recipes, at the end of this book, includes the Cholesterol-Saturated Fat Index (CSI). This is a figure that indicates the concentration of cholesterol and saturated fat in foods. It is especially useful since it is an indication of the two types of fat that need to be reduced in the American diet. These fats are saturated fat and cholesterol.

The lower the CSI number, the better the food choice is for the prevention of heart disease. A book that will give you more information on the Cholesterol-Saturated Fat Index and a listing of the CSI for many foods is *The New American Diet System* by S.L. Conner and W.E. Conner, published by Simon and Schuster, New York, 1991.

# FOOD EXCHANGES
# FOR DIABETES AND WEIGHT LOSS

Exchange lists or food groups are commonly used in many weight loss programs and in planning diabetic diets. There are six food groups or exchange lists. In forming the exchange lists, foods with similar calories, carbohydrate, protein, and fat are grouped together.

The six exchange lists are: milk, starch, meat, fruits, vegetables, and fat.

By following a meal pattern based on the exchange lists, one can "exchange" a food in one group for another food in the same group. This method helps to increase variety while at the same time keeping calories and nutrient values consistent.

Each recipe in this book has the exchanges listed. The figures used to calculate the exchanges are from the 1986 revised Exchange Lists for Meal Planning by the American Diabetes Association and American Dietetic Association. For more information on the exchange lists, contact a registered dietitian or your local Amercian Diabetes Association.

Unless otherwise noted, the calories listed for each recipe are within 20 calories of the combined caloric value of the exchanges listed after each recipe. Many of the chicken and fish recipes in this book have a notation that the calories are less than the exchanges would compute. This is because the fat content of the fish and chicken used in the recipes is lower than the fat figure (3 grams per ounce) used for the lean meat group in the exchange lists. Please be aware that the calories, carbohydrate, protein, and fat used for each exchange list are averages and are not always the exact values for a specific food within the exchange list.

Recipes with less than 20 calories per serving are usually listed as "free."

# SODIUM

Americans consume far more salt than what they need.  The American Heart Association and the American Diabetes Association recommend limiting sodium to no more than 3000 mg. per day.  People on sodium restricted diets are usually limited to 2000 mg. or less per day.

It is not always easy to reduce your sodium intake because the change in taste does take time to get used to. Start by limiting salt used at the table and then start reducing the amount you use in cooking. Salt free seasonings (such as Parsley Patch) and salt substitutes may also be used to add flavor and keep the sodium low.

The sodium content for each recipe is listed in the Nutrient Analysis of Recipes. All of the recipes are less than 800 mg. of sodium with the exception of Sausage & Sauerkraut which should be omitted by people on sodium restricted diets.

In the Nutrient Analysis of Recipes you'll find many have the sodium listed for regular, Swanson's 30 percent less salt, and salt free broth.  If only a small amount of regular broth is used in a recipe, you'll find that it does not make the recipe excessively high in sodium.

Regular soy sauce is used in these recipes but the amount is small to limit the sodium.  I have found that regular soy sauce, diluted with an equal amount of water, has a better flavor and less sodium than the lite soy sauce you can purchase.

Salt is listed as an optional ingredient in the recipes and is therefore not included in the Nutrient Analysis of Recipes.

Vegetables canned without salt should be used when available to keep the sodium content low.

# TIPS FOR REDUCING FAT AND CHOLESTEROL IN YOUR DIET

**Whether you want to lose weight, lower your cholesterol, or just be healthy, limiting the fat and cholesterol in your diet is important. The following tips are recommended for the entire family. Keep in mind that children can develop healthy eating habits if the example is provided in the home.**

- ♥ Choose lean cuts of meat, fish, and poultry. Trim off all visible fat. Animal fat is saturated fat and should be limited.

- ♥ Avoid deep-fried foods or, at least, limit how often you have them.

- ♥ Cook by baking, broiling, poaching, steaming, or microwaving.

- ♥ Avoid frying or sautéing in oil or other fats. Instead, use a non-stick spray coating or a broth.

- ♥ Eat seafood three times a week. Try more tuna fish and salmon salad sandwiches for lunch.

- ♥ Limit red meats to three times a week. Serve smaller portions (3-4 ounces).

- ♥ Increase the use of poultry, without the skin. Chicken parts can be skinned and then breaded and baked. This is a good low fat substitute for fried chicken.

- ♥ Use egg substitutes or egg whites. Limit egg yolks to three per week.

- ♥ Switch to skim or 1% milk.

- ♥ Try salad dressings that are labeled nonfat or reduced calorie.

♥ Use reduced calorie mayonnaise.

♥ Enjoy nonfat yogurts.

♥ Use tuna packed in water.

♥ Use more dried beans and dried peas in place of meat.

♥ Limit all cheeses, especially those that are not low in fat.  Look for cheeses with less than 6 grams of fat per ounce.  Five grams of fat is equal to one teaspoon of fat.

♥ Replace butter and stick margarine with soft tub-style margarines made with canola, safflower, soybean, sunflower, or corn oil.  Look for "liquid" oil as the first ingredient.

♥ Avoid animal fats such as lard and bacon grease.

♥ Limit foods with hydrogenated or partially hydrogenated oils. Hydrogenation is a chemical process that turns unsaturated liquid oils into saturated solids.

♥ Increase the use of foods that are low in saturated fats such as fruits, vegetables, and grains.

♥ Use canola oil (Puritan or Canola West) or olive oil.

♥ Limit high fat meats such as hot dogs, salami, bologna, bacon, and sausage.

♥ Refrigerate soups and stews.  The fat will harden and can easily be removed.  This also works well with canned soups (except condensed cream soups).

♥ Replace condensed, canned cream soups with the cream soup mix on page 70.  You'll reduce the fat from as much as 20 grams in a 10 3/4 ounce can to 1.5 grams of fat in an equal amount of the reconstituted mix.

♥ Instead of adding margarine to vegetables, add Molly McButter or seasonings such as Parsley Patch. For baked potatoes add 1 table-spoon of milk for moisture before sprinkling with Molly McButter.

♥ Replace sour cream with nonfat yogurt. If you don't like the flavor, use light sour cream but limit the amount used as it still contains fat.

♥ Use fruit ices and nonfat sherbets to replace ice cream.

♥ Read labels and avoid products that contain coconut oil, palm oil, and cocoa butter. These are saturated fats.

♥ Look for grams of fat on the label and choose those foods with less than 30% of the total calories from fat. To do this:

1. Find the grams of fat per serving and multiply by 9 to get the total calories from fat. There are 9 calories per gram of fat.

2. Find the calories per serving.

3. Divide the total calories from fat by the total calories per serving.

4. The answer is the percent of calories from fat.

Example: If one serving is 200 calories and has 5 grams of fat:

5 grams of fat x 9 calories per gram = 45 calories from fat

45 calories from fat ÷ 200 total calories = 23% calories from fat

By choosing foods with less than 30% of their total calories from fat, you are closer to your goal of having your total fat intake less than 30% of your total calories. Note that the percent of fat listed on foods may be by weight and *not* a percent of the total calories. This is usually the case with raw meats, milk, and ice cream.

♥ Limit your total fat intake to no more than 30% of your total daily calories with saturated fat being no more than 10% of this. This may be difficult to figure on your own but can easily be done with the help of a registered dietitian. The following may be helpful.

30% of 1200 Calories = 40 grams; 20% = 27 grams

30% of 1500 Calories = 50 grams; 20% = 33 grams

30% of 1800 Calories = 60 grams; 20% = 40 grams

30% of 2000 Calories = 67 grams; 20% = 44 grams

30% of 2500 Calories = 83 grams; 20% = 56 grams

# PRODUCTS WORTH TRYING

We live in a time where there are many excellent products being developed to meet consumers' demands. Many of these are low in calories and low in fat. More products are appearing that are also low in sodium.

I've listed some products here, with a brief description, that I think are worth trying. Although I may mention brand names there are probably other brands with similar nutrient composition. Continue to compare the nutrient information on labels as more healthy products will be arriving on the grocery shelves.

**Seltzer Water** - There are several brands sweetened with NutraSweet. These remind me of a "sophisticated" diet soda. Raspberry is my favorite flavor. WinterBrook and New York are two brands but check the labels for the sugar-free version.

**Marukan Seasoned Gourmet Rice Vinegar Lite Dressing** - You'll find this in the Oriental section of the grocery store. It is a sweetened vinegar that is good on salads or as a vegetable marinade. One tablespoon contains 16 calories, no fat, and 350 mg. of sodium. For a low sodium, sugar-free version, see the recipe "Salt Free Sweetened Rice Vinegar" in this book.

**Milani 1890 Dill Cooking Sauce & Marinade** - This is excellent as a marinade or to baste poultry, fish, or red meat. If you like dill, you'll like this product. Two ounces contain 4 calories.

**Molly McButter** - This is available in several flavors. Butter flavored is my favorite. It is great sprinkled on vegetables. One half teaspoon contains 4 calories and 90 mg. of sodium.

**Non-stick Cooking Sprays** - Several brands are available. Use for frying lean meats and vegetables without adding a lot of calories from fat.

**Mustard Mayonnaise by The Mustard Farm** - This comes in regular and low fat. I recommend the low fat version in the light blue label. One tablespoon contains 32 calories, 0 cholesterol, and 96 mg. of sodium. This is great on sandwiches.

**Reduced Calorie Mayonnaise** - Several brands are available. This product may be labeled as "imitation" or "lite." Use in place of regular mayonnaise. One tablespoon contains about 50 calories. I prefer Best Foods Light and Miracle Whip Light.

**Nonfat Yogurts** - These are available under several brand names. Some are sweetened with sugar and some are sweetened with NutraSweet. Calories vary from 80 to 150 for 6-8 ounces. My favorite is Yoplait Light.

**Swanson's Broths** - These have a good flavor and can replace homemade broth. However, they contain a significant amount of sodium. Try the chicken broth with 30% less salt.

**Salad Dressings** - Many are now available that are low in fat or are fat free. Compare labels and have a variety at home.

**Bernstein's Reduced Calorie Dressings** - These have a greast taste but limit the amount used to limit the sodium.

**Frozen T.V. Dinners** - There are numerous brands available that provide low fat and low calorie choices. When choosing a T.V. dinner, look for those with less than 800 mg. of sodium, and fat limited to no more than 30% of the calories (see page 13 for figuring fat). Most are about 300 calories so fat should be 10 grams or less. Keep some on hand for emergencies.

**Frozen Dessert Bars** - Look for those with 80 calories or less. Some are sweetened with sugar, while some are sweetened with NutraSweet. Avoid those that contain palm oil or coconut oil. Crystal Light Popsicles only contain 14 calories!

**Crystal Light Beverage** - The lemon-lime is very good and is a refreshing drink on a hot day. This product is sweetened with NutraSweet.

**Quick Cooking Brown Rice** - Cooks in only 14 minutes!

**Sugar-Free Hot Cocoa Mix**- Several are available that are 80 calories or less per cup. These are sweetened with NutraSweet and are very low in fat.

**Krusteaz Oat Bran Lite Complete Pancake Mix**- This is a good, low fat pancake mix. Three pancakes (prepared according to package directions) contain 130 calories, 10 grams of dietary fiber, 1 gram of fat, 0 cholesterol, and 370 mg. of sodium.

**Egg Beaters** - This product is found in the frozen food section. Each 8 oz. container is equivalent to 4 eggs. One fourth of a cup is equivalent to 1 egg and contains 25 calories, 0 fat, 0 cholesterol, and 80 mg. of sodium. I prefer this brand because it tastes good and does not contain any fat.

**Ragu Homestyle 100% Natural Spaghetti Sauce** - This is a low fat sauce with a good flavor. Four ounces contain 70 calories, 0 cholesterol, 2 grams of fat, and 390 mg. of sodium.

**Ragu 100% Natural Pizza Sauce** - Three tablespoons contain 25 calories, 1 gram of fat and 0 cholesterol. Great for a quick pizza!

**Vegetarian Refried Beans** - Soybean oil replaces the lard. Rosarita brand provides 100 calories, 2 grams of fat, 0 cholesterol, and 470 mg. of sodium for 4 ounces.

**Light Philadelphia Brand Pasteurized Process Cream Cheese Product** - This is available in a tub. It is a good replacement for cream cheese as it contains half the fat. One ounce contains 60 calories, 5 grams of fat, 15 mg. of cholesterol, and 160 mg. of sodium.

**Ground Turkey** - Look for packages that list 7% fat. Armour is one brand name to search for. This is a better choice than most of the frozen ground turkey which contains 15% fat.

**Ground Beef** - Most grocery stores now have ground beef available with 9% or less fat. This is a better choice over the extra lean which contains 15% fat.

**Louis Rich Smoked Turkey Sausage** - This looks like and tastes like Polish keilbasa but it is much lower in fat. One ounce contains 40 calories, 2 grams of fat, 15 mg. of cholesterol, and 250 mg. of sodium. It is still high in sodium, so limit the amount.

**Canola Oil** - This oil contains the least amount of saturated fat and the most amount of monosaturated fat. Puritan and Canola West are a couple of brand names. Olive oil is also high in monosaturated fats and is a good choice.

**Kikkoman Soy Sauce** - I prefer the taste of the regular diluted with an equal amount of water over the taste of the lite. Also the sodium is lower in the diluted version. One fourth teaspoon of the regular, diluted with an equal amount of water, is 1 calorie and 80 mg. of sodium. One half teaspoon of the lite is 2 calories and 100 mg. of sodium.

**Cheeses** - Many low fat varieties are now on the market. I prefer to buy 2-pound bricks of part skim milk mozzarella, and Kraft Light Naturals (a cheddar cheese with 1/3 less fat). However, they still need to be limited as both contain a fair amount of fat. One ounce is about 80 calories, 5 grams of fat, 20 mg. of cholesterol, and 180 mg. of sodium.

**Laughing Cow Reduced Calorie Cheese Product** - This product comes in a round green container. Each one ounce wedge contains 3 grams of fat, 50 calories, and 370 mg. of sodium. It is a soft cheese that is easy to spread on a cracker. You'll like this product if you like Brie cheese.

**Chopped or Minced Garlic** - This is available in the produce section of the grocery store. Use 1/2 tsp. in place of one garlic clove.

**Dried Chopped Onion** - This is sold with seasonings and herbs. Use 2 Tbl. to replace 1/2 cup chopped raw onion. Reconstitute in water or use as is.

**Schilling's Parsley Patch** - A good salt free seasoning which is an herb and spice blend.

**Canned Soups** - Progresso and Campbell have several good soups on the market that are low in fat. Some of the chunky versions make a good meal with the addition of bread. Check the label for sodium. Choose soups with less than 30% of the calories from fat. See page 13 for figuring the fat.

**Frozen Vegetables** - Keep a few packages on hand. The vegetable combinations, without sauces, are usually a good choice. These work well as a side dish, in soups and stews, or in stir-fry dishes.

**Low-fat canned chilies** - Note that the sodium is high and should be avoided by those on sodium restricted diets. Figures are for 1/2 can.

**Cimmaron Chicken Chili with Beans** (5 grams of fat (25% fat), 180 calories, 970 mg. sodium)

**Stagg Chicken Chili with Beans** (7 grams of fat (32% fat), 200 calories, sodium not listed)

**Cimmaron Beef Chili with Beans, Mild** (8 grams of fat (31% fat), 230 calories, sodium not listed)

**Fred Meyer Chili Con Carne with Beans** (9 grams of fat (31% fat), 260 calories, 770 mg. sodium)

**Nalley Chili Con Carne with Beans** (10 grams of fat (33% fat), 270 calories, 950 mg. of sodium)

# TIME SAVING IDEAS

**Here are some ideas that I have found helpful to reduce my time in the kitchen.**

■ Cleaning and chopping vegetables can be a time consuming task. I prefer to do whole packages at one time and refrigerate in sealed plastic bags. However, you can purchase cleaned and cut vegetables which may be worth it if you cannot, or will not, take the time to prepare the fresh vegetables. You can even buy cleaned and chopped lettuce for salads. Check grocery stores and Deli's for these. If this is the only way you will include fresh vegetables in your diet, do it!

■ One of the lowest calorie, best tasting, and quickest ways of preparing vegetables is to cook them in your microwave (without any sauces). You don't need a detailed recipe, just consult your microwave cookbook for cooking times.

■ A salad spinner is a must to make cleaning lettuce a quick task. I usually will do a whole head of lettuce and store in sealed plastic bags.

■ Buy packages of cleaned stir-fry vegetables, and meat or poultry already cut for stir-frying.

■ You can buy low fat grated cheese in most grocery stores but the cost is about twice as much as the brick form. Grating cheese is easy in a food processor, but only worth it if you are doing a large amount. I grate two 2-pound bricks (usually one of mozzarella and one of Kraft Light Natural) at a time and freeze for future use. Home grated cheese can be lighter than the store bought grated cheese and goes further as a topping in a recipe. As a result you get less fat and less calories when topping the same area with home-grated cheese.

**General Rule: Purchased grated: 4 oz. equals 1 cup**
**Home Grated: 2 oz. equals 1 cup**

You can weigh a cup of your home grated cheese to see how much you get. Recipes in this book use ounces of cheese instead of cups.

- Keep staple foods on hand so that you always have the ingredients for several meals.

- Find a convenient place in your kitchen for a grocery list that family members can add to. Encourage them to add items when they are low and not empty.

- Plan meals for the next week and add items needed to the grocery list before shopping.

- Grocery shop from your list once a week and avoid stops at the grocery store after work.

- Double a recipe and freeze for future meals.

- Buy skinned and boned chicken breasts in the family pack and freeze. Ask your butcher to package lean meats in a family pack since this usually means less cost to you. Of course, you'll have to divide the package into meal size portions and freeze.

- Look for packages of frozen lean meats and poultry that are already portioned.

- Buy a turkey breast and have the butcher slice it into steaks for use in place of chicken breasts. Freeze with two pieces of wax paper between slices for easy removal.

- To skin chicken parts, place a paper towel on the skin and pull.

- Purchase chopped garlic and substitute it for the fresh.

- Use dried onion instead of chopping fresh. See the label for reconstituting for certain recipes.

# CONTROLLING YOUR WEIGHT

**Whether you want to lose weight or maintain your present weight it may be helpful for you to follow some of these tips.**

## ■ EXERCISE ON A REGULAR BASIS

Choose an aerobic exercise that you enjoy, such as walking. Start walking for 5 minutes and gradually work up to 30 minutes.

Plan on exercising *at least* three times a week. It not only will help you to burn calories, but it also motivates you to continue to work at good food choices. It also makes you feel great!

Incorporate more exercise into your day. Use stairs instead of elevators, park your car at a distance from your destination, etc.

## ■ BECOME A PLANNER

Plan meals in advance.

Plan on grocery shopping when you are not hungry so you can stick to your list. Shop once a week.

Keep low calorie foods on hand and keep high calorie foods out of the house.

Think about social gatherings in advance and have a plan to help you be in control. Never go to a party hungry!

Plan meals with variety so you don't get bored.

Be prepared for problem times and emergencies.

Plan on not skipping meals because you'll overeat at your next meal or you'll snack and end up eating more calories.

## ■ LEARN ABOUT GOOD FOOD CHOICES

Seek out reliable information on low fat and low calorie foods.

Change your cooking methods and recipes to low fat.

Learn more about calories and/or food exchange groups.

Read labels and avoid foods that are high in calories and low in nutrients.

## ■ LIMIT PORTION SIZES

Measuring foods can help you to limit your serving sizes. Three ounces of meat, about the size of a deck of cards, is an adequate portion.

Serve food from the stove and not in bowls at the table. This may help you to avoid "just one more spoonful."

Cook only the amount you need to avoid the temptation of seconds.

Ask your family to clear their own plates and to put away any leftovers. Try using a smaller plate.

Drop out of the Clean Plate Club.

Leave the table immediately after eating if you are tempted to eat more.

## ■ ENJOY EATING

Don't eat absentmindedly. Make a conscious decision to eat.

Eat slowly and relish each bite. You'll probably eat less.

Choose only one or two locations in the house for eating.

Do no other activity while eating. Take time to enjoy.

## ■ KEEP A DAILY EATING RECORD

Write it down before you eat it. You'll think more about your choices.

Review your record at the end of the day for good points.

Dwell on the positive, not the negative.

■ **STORE FOOD OUT OF SIGHT**
Never leave food on the counter.

Store tempting foods in inconvenient places.

Spend less time in places and situations where you are surrounded by food.

Avoid buying foods that are too tempting for you to resist.

At work, do not eat at your desk.

■ **IGNORE SOCIAL PRESSURES**
Don't feel compelled to eat.

Enjoy the conversation and company more than the food.

Keep your back to buffet tables at parties.

■ **THINK POSITIVE**
Picture yourself as you want to look.

Use positive self-talk every day.

Live your thin life now and you will succeed. Don't put things off until you lose weight.

■ **DON'T BE AN EMOTION EATER**
Find other avenues to vent your feelings such as bubble baths, walks, or calling a friend.

Seek professional counseling to help you better deal with your problems.

■ **CONTROL SNACKING**
Choose healthy snacks, such as fresh fruit, and limit the amounts.

If you snack while cooking, substitute chewing gum or drinking water.

Try a flavored hot or iced tea for an evening snack.

## ■ DON'T EAT JUST FOR SOMETHING TO DO
Search out hobbies and friends.

Plan activities for the time you usually spend snacking.

## ■ DRINK WATER
Drink at least 2 quarts of fluids every day.  Your best choice is water.

Limit fruit juices since they are high in calories.

## ■ FORGET THE SCALE
Remember the scale can be discouraging because it does not separate water from muscle or fat.

Measure your success by the positive changes you have made in eating and exercise.  These changes, if continued, will bring about permanent weight control.

## ■ BE REALISTIC
Reduce, don't eliminate, favorite foods.  Moderation is the key to success, even with high calorie foods.

Make changes gradually.  Choose one thing to work on this week.

Don't give up if you have a bad day.  We all have those once in awhile.  Be determined to succeed.

Learn from your mistakes instead of allowing them to make you feel like a failure.  We all make mistakes.

## ■ SET REALISTIC GOALS
A 1-2 pound loss per week is a good weight loss.

Set an ideal weight that is attainable.  You don't have to be skinny.

## ■ ALLOW YOURSELF REWARDS
Try a manicure or something other than food.

Go window shopping.

## ■ LOOK TO A PROFESSIONAL FOR SUPPORT
Get support to help you make the changes you need to succeed.

Avoid fad diets and programs that attract you with their promise of fast weight loss. You'll only gain the weight back.

Seek out the help of a registered dietitian, a professional who has the educational background to give you the sound advice and support you need.

## ■ KEEP THE WEIGHT OFF
Don't give up after you reach your goal and regain the weight. Remember, 20 years of poor habits take more than a few months to change.

Be willing to work at controlling your weight the rest of your life!

# IDEAS FOR QUICK MEALS AND SNACKS

**Here are some quick ideas that do not require a detailed recipe.**

## ■ BREAKFAST

Spread a thin layer of old-fashioned peanut butter on whole wheat toast.

Top a bagel with Light Philadelphia Cream Cheese Product or Laughing Cow Reduced Calorie Cheese Product.

Make a breakfast yogurt by mixing nonfat yogurt with fresh fruit and a cereal such as Grapenuts.

Make pancakes with Krusteaz Oat Bran Lite Complete Pancake Mix.

Use non-stick cooking spray for cooking pancakes, French toast, and eggs.

Try low sugar jam on toast, pancakes, or French toast to replace the margarine and/or syrup.  Applesauce is also good on pancakes.

Serve low fat cottage cheese with fruit.

Make a breakfast pizza by toasting an English muffin half and topping with Ragu 100% Natural Pizza Sauce and 1/2 ounce of part skim mozzarella cheese.  Broil until cheese melts.

Make an omelet with egg substitute and top with salsa.  Also try it with mushrooms or other vegetables.

Serve a whole grain cereal, with less than 3 grams of fat per serving, with skim milk and fresh fruit.

Try whole wheat toast with low sugar jam and one of the shakes in this book.

# ■ SANDWICHES

Fill pita bread with raw vegetables and tuna salad or lean sliced turkey.

Spread melba toast with Laughing Cow Reduced Calorie Cheese Product.

Top a rice cake with low fat Ricotta cheese and salsa, or omit the salsa and sprinkle with cinnamon and sweetener.

Use whole, canned green chiles in turkey sandwiches, omitting mayonnaise or margarine.

Spread a thin layer of Laughing Cow Reduced Calorie Cheese Product or Light Philadelphia Brand Pasteurized Process Cream Cheese Product on whole wheat bread or a bagel instead of using margarine or mayonnaise. Melt in microwave if desired.  Add a thin slice of smoked turkey.

Fill pita bread with the stir-fry recipe or fajita recipe in this book.

Microwave (or cook in a skillet with non-stick cooking spray) a skinned and boned chicken breast and serve on a bun. Top with lettuce and a tomato slice or with barbecue sauce.

Try tuna salad made with water packed tuna and reduced calorie mayonnaise. For more flavor add 1 tablespoon of pickle relish or diced green chiles. Celery can also be added for crunch.  Chopped apple is a good addition to add sweetness and a crunch.

Make tuna salad with low calorie ranch dressing.

Make a submarine sandwich using lean meats and chopped lettuce. Drizzle with nonfat or reduced calorie Italian dressing.

Add well drained coleslaw to a sandwich for crunch.

Make a reuben sandwich using whole wheat toast, smoked turkey, part-skim mozzarella cheese, and rinsed sauerkraut. Heat under broiler until cheese is melted.

Use lettuce and tomato in sandwiches for moisture and to replace mayonnaise or margarine.

Make a French dip using deli roast beef or turkey, French rolls, and French's Au Jus Gravy Mix (dilute with more water to reduce the sodium).

Try alfalfa sprouts in place of lettuce. You don't have to wash them and they have less of a tendency to get soggy.

# ■ LUNCH AND DINNER

Make a cold plate in the summer of sliced fresh fruit with low fat cottage cheese or sliced lean meats, low fat cheese, and vegetables.

Top tossed salads with kidney or garbanzo beans.

Fill heated tortillas with vegetarian refried beans or black beans and top with salsa. Serve with nonfat yogurt, chopped lettuce and tomatoes.

Fill a baked potato with low fat cottage cheese and chopped green onion or black beans and salsa.

Top a baked potato with one of the canned chilies listed on page 19. Add chopped onion but be cautious when adding cheese.

Serve one of the canned chilies listed on page 19. Top with sliced green onion and serve with French bread and carrot sticks.

Make a shish-ka-bob of green peppers, onion, and partially cooked new potato quarters. Skewer with cubes of lean meat, poultry, or shrimp. Broil or barbeque until done.

Serve spaghetti using Ragu 100% Natural Spaghetti Sauce and eggless noodles.

When making macaroni and cheese from the box, use skim milk and omit (or at least reduce) the margarine.

Use a broth-based canned soup (not cream) and skim off the fat. To reduce the sodium, add additional water, purchase those that indicate they are 30% less salt (Campbell has several), or mix with a low sodium soup. When selecting a thicker soup, choose those with less than 30% of the calories from fat. See page 13 for figuring fat.

Serve a frozen T.V. dinner with less than 30% of the calories from fat (i.e., 300 calories-10 grams of fat) and less than 800 mg. of sodium. See page 13 for figuring fat.

Dress up green beans with mushrooms and slivered almonds.

Make a stir-fry using lean meat, seafood, or poultry and add a couple of fresh vegetables.

When serving meat, poultry or seafood, complete the meal with a roll and either canned, frozen or a fresh vegetable. Using the microwave makes this especially fast.

# ■ DESSERTS

Top angel food cake with fresh fruit and lite whipped topping.

Make a frozen dessert of angel food cake and nonfat frozen yogurt by slicing the cake horizontally into 3 layers and spreading softened frozen yogurt between each layer. Freeze until serving.

Serve frozen fruit bars.  Look for those with less than 80 calories, and no fat. People with diabetes should also look for those without sugar.

Layer sugar-free Jello with sugar-free pudding in parfait glasses.

Fill the center of half a cantaloupe with sugar-free Jello and refrigerate until set. Cut in half before serving.

Drizzle nonfat lemon yogurt over sugar-free Jello.

Frost a cake with lite whipped topping.  Use the Cream Cheese Topping in this book for a filling between layers.  For additional flavor, spread crushed pineapple over the Cream Cheese Topping.

# ■ SNACKS

air popped popcorn

pretzels (you can buy unsalted)

rice cakes with low sugar jam

fresh fruit

herbal teas

nonfat yogurt, plain or fruit flavored

raw vegetables

tomato juice (can buy unsalted)

sugar-free hot cocoa

vanilla wafers, gingersnaps, graham crackers, animal crackers, fig bars

unsalted top saltine crackers, RyKrisp (unseasoned), ak-mak, Bremner wafers, melba toast

sugar-free flavored seltzer waters such as WinterBrook or New York Diet

# DINNER MENUS

Here are fifty simple dinner menus. The recipes in this book are marked with an asterisk. Although milk is not listed, it would be a good addition to any meal. Adjust portion sizes to meet your caloric needs.

Italian Cioppino*
French Roll

Yogurt Cumin Chicken*
Fresh Carrots (microwave or raw)
Refried Beans*

Tortilla Pie*
Orange Wedges
Sliced Tomatoes

Italian Zucchini Frittata*
Toasted Bagel

Clam Fettucini*
Tossed Salad

Stir-Fry: Chicken*
Angel Hair Pasta

Orange Pork Chops*
Microwave Baked Potato*
Fresh Broccoli (microwave)

Chili Con Carne*
Raw Vegetable Sticks
Unsalted Top Saltine Crackers

Oven Fried Fish/Oysters*
Oven Fried French Fries*
Cabbage Salad*

Chicken and Spinach Salad*
Italian Focaccia Bread*

Puffy Chili Relleno Casserole*
Spanish Yogurt Sauce*
Sliced Cucumbers
Sliced Fruit

Boboli Pizza-Sausage or Shrimp*
Italian Herb Tomatoes*

Chinese Pepper Steak*
Quick Cooking Brown Rice

Vegetables Primavera*
Bagel Half spread with Laughing
   Cow Reduced Calorie Cheese

Fillets of Sole Thermador*
Broccoli and Carrots (microwave)
Whole Wheat Roll

Chicken Breasts Florentine*
Herb and Vegetable Rice Blend*

John Torrey*
Seasoned Green Beans*

Minestrone Soup*
French Roll with Laughing
   Cow Reduced Calorie Cheese

Combination Salad Plate:
   Curry Tuna Salad*
   Fiesta Salad*
Oat Bran Muffin*

Mexican Chicken Casserole*
Thick and Chunky Salsa*
Raw Vegetable Sticks
Sliced Fruit

Ground Meat and Mushroom -Potato
   Topping*
Marinated Vegetables*

Sweet Mustard Fish*
Mexican Vegetables*
Hot Roll

Quick Lasagna*
Tossed Salad

Three Bean Soup*
French Bread
Yoplait Light (or any nonfat yogurt)

French Glazed Chicken*
Microwave Baked Potato*
Greek Salad*

Sausage and Sauerkraut*
Fruit Salad*

Marinated Steak*
Microwave Baked Potato*
Tossed Salad

Lemon Fish*
Fresh Cucumber Sauce*
Broccoli Salad*
Hot Roll

Oven Fried Chicken*
Ranch Beans*
Gourmet Cucumbers*

Tomato and Basil Pasta*
Low Fat Cottage Cheese
Sliced Fruit

Fish Stew*
Whole Wheat Roll

Swedish Meatballs*
Mashed Potatoes
Asparagus (microwave)

Chicken Breasts Supreme*
Fettucini Noodles
Mixed Vegetables

Turkey French Dip*
Basil Tomatoes*

Oriental Rice & Seafood Salad*
Refrigerator Bran Muffin*

Chicken Enchiladas*
Spanish Yogurt Dressing*
Raw Vegetable Sticks
Sliced Orange

Pork Chop Suey*
Quick Cooking Brown Rice

Crusty Calzone*
Tossed Salad

Baked Fish with Bottled Topping*
Cheese Stuffed Potato*
Cauliflower & Broccoli (microwave)

Meat Patties*
Hamburger Bun
Tomato/Lettuce
Raw Vegetable Sticks

Mexican Style Chicken and Rice*
Sliced Fruit

New England Fish Chowder*
Vegetable Bean Salad*
Whole Wheat Roll

Cold Plate:
    Sliced Lean Deli Meats and
    Low Fat Cheese
    Lentil Rice Salad*

Spaghetti and Meatballs*
Tossed Salad

Chicken and Pea Pod Stir-Fry*
Herb Rice Blend*

Seafood Salad on Toasted English
    Muffin*
Apple Salad Mold*

Pizza-Potato Topping*
Sliced Cucumbers

Oriental Noodle Soup*
Turkey Sandwich
Raw Vegetable Sticks

Beef or Pork Fajitas*
Sliced Tomato and Lettuce

Polynesian Chicken*
Quick Cooking Brown Rice
Zucchini, Tomato & Onions*
Pineapple Chunks

# GROCERY LISTS

This section includes a list of staples, perishables, and a weekly grocery list. All of the recipes in this book and almost everything in the sections "Ideas for Quick Meals and Snacks" and "Dinner Menus" can be prepared if these food items are on hand.

The staple grocery list has items that have a longer shelf life. Many of these may already be in your home. You may prefer to purchase in larger quantities so you won't have to shop for these items weekly. It's a good idea to add to your weekly grocery list any item taken from the cupboard or freezer. Don't wait until you are out of the item.

Perishables are listed separately and consist of fresh foods that have a shorter shelf life. However, some of these items, such as bread, can be frozen and therefore can be purchased in larger quantities.

Make copies of both the staples and perishables grocery lists. Either take them with you when you shop or use them to complete the Weekly Grocery List. It can also serve as a good reminder of the basics needed for a week.

Extra copies of all grocery lists can be found on pages 251-260.

# WEEKLY GROCERY LIST

**Milk/Yogurt/Cheese/Eggs**

_____

_____

_____

**Canned & Packaged Foods**

_____

_____

_____

**Breads & Cereals**

_____

_____

_____

**Frozen Foods**

_____

_____

_____

**Fresh Vegetables**
(choose for salad or raw and 2 for
cooking)

_____

_____

_____

**Fresh Fruit** (2-3)

_____

_____

_____

**Meat/Poultry/Seafood**

_____

_____

_____

**Sandwich/Lunch Makings**

_____

_____

_____

**Miscellaneous**

_____

_____

_____

_____

_____

_____

Choose an entreé for each main meal and check ingredients needed and add
them to this list.

# GROCERY LIST: STAPLES

## Spices and Baking Products
allspice
dried basil
bay leaves
celery seed
chili powder
dried cilantro
cinnamon
ground cloves
coriander
cumin
curry
dried dill
garlic powder
ginger
Italian herb seasoning
Kitchen Bouquet
liquid smoke
dried marjoram
nutmeg
dried onion
dried oregano
onion powder
paprika
dried parsley
dry mustard (Colemans)
pepper
poppy seeds
poultry seasoning
dried rosemary
salt/Lite salt/salt substitute
sesame seeds
tabasco sauce
dried tarragon
dried thyme

Worcestershire Sauce
bacon soy bits
Molly McButter (natural butter)
Parsley Patch Salt Free Sea-
    soning
taco seasoning
almond extract
maple extract
rum extract
vanilla extract
unbleached flour
whole wheat flour
cornstarch
cocoa
baking powder
baking soda
granulated sugar
Equal sweetener
brown sugar or
    brown sugar substitute
powdered sugar
honey (optional)
molasses
nonfat dry milk
cornflake crumbs
canola oil (Puritan or Canola
    West)
olive oil
non-stick cooking spray
Krusteaz Oat Bran Lite Pancake
    Mix
sugar-free instant vanilla pudding
    mix
sugar-free cherry Jello
sugar-free lime Jello

walnuts (optional)

## Canned Oriental Foods
bean sprouts
chinese-style vegetables
water chestnuts
soy sauce (Kikkoman)
Marukan Seasoned Gourmet
    Rice Vinegar Lite Dressing
    or Marukan Rice Vinegar

## Canned Mexican Foods
whole green chiles
diced green chiles
salsa, thick and chunky
enchilada sauce
vegetarian refried beans

## Canned and Packaged Fruits
crushed pineapple (natural
    juice)
pineapple chunks (natural juice)
mandarin oranges
applesauce, unsweetened
lite cherry pie filling (Wilderness
    brand)
lemon juice
lime juice
raisins
dates

## Canned Vegetables and Legumes

*\* use "no salt added" if available*
artichoke hearts
tomato sauce\*
tomato paste
canned tomatoes\*
stewed tomatoes\*
tomato juice\*
sauerkraut
sliced/chopped mushrooms\*
pimento
green beans\*
whole kernel corn\*
creamed corn
vegetarian baked beans
garbanzo beans\*
kidney beans\*
black eyed peas\*
pinto beans\*
chilies (with beans):
    Cimmaron Chicken Chili
    Cimmaron Beef Chili
    Stagg Chicken Chili
    Nalley Chili Con Carne
    Fred Meyer Chili Con Carne

## Dressings, Sauces, Jams and Vinegar

reduced calorie mayonnaise
    (Best Foods Lite)
mustard mayonnaise (Mustard
    Farm-low fat)
Miracle Whip Lite
ranch style dressing mix
    (buttermilk type)
French's Au Jus Gravy Mix
low calorie French dressing

low calorie Italian dressing
    (Bernsteins)
chili sauce
seafood cocktail sauce
catsup
Dijon mustard
Roger Hong's Chinese Barbecue
    Sauce
Coleman's Hot English Mustard
S & W Mesquite Cooking Sauce
    & Marinade
Lea & Perrins White Wine
    Worcestershire Sauce
Kraft Sauceworks Sweet'n Sour
    Sauce
Old Spice Honey Mustard
Milani 1890 Dill Sauce
low sugar apricot jam
low sugar orange marmalade
vinegar
red wine vinegar
malt vinegar
Ragu Homestyle Spaghetti
    Sauce ( meatless)
Ragu 100% Natural Pizza
    Sauce

## Frozen Foods

chopped spinach
pea pods
peas
Oriental style vegetables (plain)
blueberries
strawberries
orange juice concentrate
Crystal Lite Popsicles
Egg Beaters (egg substitute)
bread dough

chicken breasts/ parts/turkey
    breast
ground beef (9% fat or less)
ground turkey (7% fat)
cooked, cubed chicken (diced)
cooked shrimp
fish fillets: cod, sole, snapper,
    halibut

## Produce

onions
chopped garlic
carrots
potatoes

## Pasta (eggless), Rice, and Dried Beans

elbow macaroni
angel hair pasta
fettucini noodles
lasagna noodles
spaghetti noodles
dried black eyed peas
pearl barley
dried green split peas
dried lentils
quick cooking brown rice

## Cereals, Crackers and Cookies

old fashioned or quick-cooking
    oatmeal
oat bran
Grapenuts
All Bran
Bran Buds or 100% Bran
whole grain cereals (less than 3
    grams of fat per serving)

rice cakes
melba toast
RyKrisp (unseasoned)
unsalted top saltines
vanilla wafers
gingersnaps
graham crackers,
animal crackers
fig bars

**Soups and Soup Mixes**
Swanson's beef broth
Swanson's chicken broth (30%
    less salt)
beef and chicken bouillon
    (regular or salt free)
tomato soup
chicken gumbo
dry vegetable soup mix

**Canned Seafood**
water pack tuna
minced clams
red salmon

**Beverages**
sugar-free hot cocoa mix
sugar-free soda pop:
    Fresca or Sprite
    cream, orange
sugar-free seltzer: raspberry
    (WinterBrook or New York)
apple juice
herbal teas
Crystal Light, lemon-lime

**Miscellaneous**
peanut butter
pop corn
pretzels (available unsalted)
Parmesan cheese
dry sherry
dry white wine or vermouth

# GROCERY LIST: PERISHABLES

### Breads and Grains

(choose several)
whole wheat bread
English muffins
hamburger buns
Pita bread
French rolls
Focaccia bread
Boboli Italian bread shell
French bread
flour tortillas (6" size)
corn tortillas

### Dairy and Cheese

milk, skim or 1%
buttermilk
nonfat yogurt, plain
sweetened nonfat yogurt
   (Yoplait Light)
lite sour cream
low fat cottage cheese
low fat Ricotta cheese
feta cheese**
Light Philadelphia Cream
   Cheese Product (tub)
Laughing Cow Reduced Calorie
   Cheese Product
part-skim mozzarella cheese
Kraft Light Naturals (1/3 less fat)
   cheddar
margarine

### Fresh Vegetables

(choose enough for salad/raw
veggies and 2 for cooking)
cucumber
green onion
lettuce
radishes
tomatoes
mushrooms
celery
peppers: green, red, yellow
broccoli
cauliflower
zucchini
cabbage
spinach
asparagus

### Fresh Fruit

(choose 2-3 in season)
apples
oranges
grapefruit
strawberries
bananas
grapes
melons

### Meats, Poultry, and Seafood

top sirloin steak
round steak
rib pork chops
fresh oysters (jar)
imitation crab
sliced turkey Deli meats
Smoked Turkey Sausage (Louis
   Rich)
also see Frozen on "Staple List"

### Miscellaneous

Pillsbury's Best Sugar Cookie
   Dough**
angel food cake

** used in only one recipe

# *B*everages

# Banana Milk Shake

Serve this as a breakfast drink or after school snack. Take advantage of bananas on sale. Freeze them in the peel and let them sit out at room temperature about ten minutes for easier peeling.

**1/2 small banana**
**1/2 cup skim milk**
**1/4 tsp. almond extract**
**2 ice cubes (optional)**
**sweetener to taste: 1 tsp. sugar or 1/2 pkt. Equal sweetener**

Blend first four ingredients until smooth. Sweeten to taste.

Yield: about 1 cup
One serving: 1 cup
Calories per serving: 90 with Equal, 105 with sugar
Exchanges: 1/2 milk, 1 fruit

# Buttermilk Fruit Shake

Buttermilk fans will enjoy this combination with fruit. Fresh peaches are especially good in this recipe.

**1/2 cup buttermilk**
**1/2 cup sliced fruit**
**1/4 tsp. vanilla extract**
**2 ice cubes**
**sweetener to taste: 1/2 to 1 pkt. Equal sweetener or 1 to 2 tsp. sugar**

Blend first four ingredients until smooth. Sweeten to taste.

Yield: about 1 cup
One serving: 1 cup
Calories per serving: 90 with Equal, 105 with sugar
Exchanges: 1/2 milk, 1 fruit

# Fruit Milk Shake

Take advantage of seasonal fresh fruit when making this recipe.

**1/2 cup skim milk**
**1/2 cup sliced fruit (peaches, strawberries, etc.)**
**2 ice cubes**
**1/2 tsp. vanilla extract**
**sweetener to taste: 1 to 2 tsp. sugar or 1/2 to 1 pkt. Equal sweetener**

Blend first four ingredients until smooth.  Sweeten to taste.

Yield: about 1 cup
One serving: 1 cup
Calories per serving: 85 with Equal, 100 with sugar
Exchanges: 1/2 milk, 1 fruit

# Orange Julius

This popular breakfast drink can also serve as a delicious after school snack.

**8 oz. nonfat plain yogurt**
**1 can (6oz.) frozen orange juice concentrate**
**2 1/2 cups skim milk**
**1 tsp. vanilla extract**

Blend all ingredients until smooth.

Yield: about 4 1/2 cups (6 servings)
One serving: 3/4 cup
Calories per serving: 115
Exchanges: 1/2 milk, 1 fruit

# Wake-Up Shake

Serve for breakfast with whole wheat toast. Take advantage of bananas on sale. Freeze them in the peel and let them sit out at room temperature about ten minutes for easier peeling.

**1 small banana**
**3/4 cup skim milk**
**1/2 cup nonfat sugar-free flavored yogurt\* (try strawberry)**
**1/4 cup orange juice**

Blend all ingredients until smooth.

Yield: about 2 cups (2 servings)
One serving: 1 cup
Calories per serving: 120
Exchanges: 1/2 milk, 1 fruit

\*Calories listed are for yogurt sweetened with NutraSweet.

# Yogurt Fruit Shake

Yogurt fans will enjoy this creamy shake.  This is great with fresh fruit but can also be made with unsweetened canned fruit.

**1/2 cup nonfat plain yogurt\***
**1/2 cup sliced fruit**
**2  ice cubes**
**1/4 tsp. vanilla extract**
**sweetener to taste: about 2 tsp. sugar or 1 pkt. Equal**

Blend first four ingredients until smooth.  Sweeten to taste.

Yield: about 1 cup
One serving: 1 cup
Calories per serving: 105 with Equal, 130 with sugar
Exchanges: Using Equal: 1/2 milk, 1 fruit
           Using sugar: 1/2 milk, 1 1/2 fruit

\*Omit sweetener if yogurt sweetened with NutraSweet is used.

# Juice Cooler

Try this recipe with orange juice and lemon soda or use other juices for variety. Garnish with lemon or lime slice.

**1/2 cup fruit juice, unsweetened**
**1 cup sugar-free soda pop (lemon lime, Sprite, tonic water, Fresca, etc.)**
**ice cubes**

Fill a tall glass with ice cubes.  Add juice and soda pop.  Stir to mix.

Yield: 1 1/2 cups
One serving: 1 1/2 cups
Calories per serving: 60
Exchanges: 1 fruit

# Wine Cooler*

Burgundy wine with Fresca combine to give a good flavor and a berry pink color.  If you prefer less sweetness, use half Fresca and half diet tonic water. Garnish with orange or lemon slice.

**1/2 cup wine (white, red or blush)**
**1 cup sugar-free soda pop (Fresca, lemon lime, gingerale, tonic water, Sprite,**
  **Club Soda, seltzer water, etc.)**
**ice cubes**

Fill a tall glass with ice cubes.  Add wine and soda pop.  Stir to mix.

Yield: 1 1/2 cups
One serving: 1 1/2 cups
Calories per serving: 90
Exchanges: 2 fat

*People with diabetes should consult their physician before using alcohol.

# Appetizers, Dressings, & Sauces

Moderation is usually the key when it comes to dressings and appetizers. Be aware of the serving size and limit yourself accordingly.

# Creamy Seafood Dip

This is a good choice for a party. Fresh shrimp or crab can be used in place of canned.

**4 oz. Light Philadelphia Cream Cheese Product (1/3 of a 12 oz. tub)**
**1 pint low fat cottage cheese**
**3 Tbl. lemon juice**
**2 tsp. prepared horseradish**
**1/4 tsp. Tabasco sauce**
**1/4 cup chopped green onion**
**1 can (6 1/2 oz.) minced clams, shrimp, or crab, drained**

Have cream cheese at room temperature. In blender or food processor, blend cheeses and next three ingredients until smooth. Stir in onions and seafood. Serve with raw vegetables or crackers.

Yield: about 3 cups (24 servings)
One serving: 2 Tbl.
Calories per serving: 30
Exchanges: 1/2 lean meat

Variation: Add 1 tsp. liquid smoke when blending ingredients.

# Mock Sour Cream

This is great on baked potatoes or as a dip for vegetables.

**1/4 cup skim milk**
**1 cup low fat cottage cheese**

Place all ingredients in blender and mix on high speed until smooth and creamy. Add seasonings, such as dill, to add flavor if this is being used as a dip.

Yield: about 1 1/4 cups (12 servings)
One serving: 2 Tbl.
Calories per serving: 15
Exchanges: 1/3 lean meat

# Smoked Salmon Spread

This is a delicious spread that even children like. Red canned salmon or left over fresh salmon work the best in this recipe. Use this spread on raw vegetables or crackers.

**1 tub (12 oz.) Light Philadelphia Cream Cheese Product**
**1/2 cup light sour cream**
**1 tsp. liquid smoke**
**1 Tbl. lemon juice**
**1 1/2 tsp. Worcestershire sauce**
**1/8 tsp. salt (optional)**
**1/8 tsp. pepper**
**1 can (15 1/2 oz.) red salmon, drained, or 2 cups cooked and flaked fresh salmon**
**2 Tbl. chopped celery**
**2 Tbl. chopped green onion**

Have cream cheese at room temperature. Remove skin from salmon and mash bones. Blend first seven ingredients in a mixer. Stir in salmon, celery and onion.

Yield: about 3 cups (24 servings)
One serving: 2 Tbl.
Calories per serving: 65
Exchanges: 1/2 lean meat, 1 fat

Variation: Liquid smoke may be omitted.

# Spinach Dip

This is a low calorie version of a favorite hors d'oeuvre. It looks impressive if you hollow a round loaf of bread and fill it with the dip. Cube the bread that you remove and use it to spread the dip on.

**1 pkg. (10 oz.) frozen chopped spinach**
**1/4  package (2 Tbl.)  dry vegetable soup mix**
**1 3/4 cups plain nonfat yogurt**
**1/4 cup reduced calorie mayonnaise**
**1 can (8 oz.) water chestnuts, drained and chopped**
**2 Tbl. chopped green onion**
**1/4 tsp. dry mustard**

Thaw spinach, drain and squeeze until dry. Stir dry soup before measuring to mix evenly. Mix all ingredients. Chill and serve with raw vegetables or slices of French or sour dough bread.

Yield: about 3 1/2 cups (14 servings)
One serving: 1/4 cup
Calories per serving: 40
Exchanges: 1 vegetable

# Low Fat Ranch Dressing

Try this low calorie version of a favorite dressing. You'll find that the taste is the same as the high calorie version but the consistency is thinner. It tastes great on salads or as a dip. If you don't like the taste of yogurt, substitute reduced calorie mayonnaise. To reduce the sodium, use the seasonings instead of the dressing mix. The difference per tablespoon is 70 mg. of sodium with the dressing mix and 28 mg. of sodium with the seasonings.

**1 package (0.4 oz.) ranch style dressing mix (the kind that calls for buttermilk)**
   *or  1 Tbl. dried onion*
      *1/4 tsp. dried basil*
      *1/4 tsp. dried thyme*
      *1/4 tsp. garlic powder*
      *1 Tbl. dried parsley*
      *1/8 tsp. pepper*
      *1/2 tsp. salt (optional)*
**1/2 cup nonfat plain yogurt**
**1/2 cup reduced calorie mayonnaise**
**1 pint buttermilk**

In large bowl, blend package (or seasonings) with yogurt and mayonnaise. Mix in buttermilk. This stores well in the refrigerator for several weeks.

Yield: 3 cups (48 servings)
One serving: 1 Tbl.
Calories per serving: 14
Exchanges: "free"

# Salt-Free Sweetened Rice Vinegar

This recipe can be used in place of the bottled Marukan Seasoned Gourmet Rice Vinegar Lite Dressing. The main difference is that one tablespoon of the bottled Lite Dressing contains 350 mg. of sodium, whereas this recipe is salt free. Also, this recipe can be made with Equal which would be a better choice for people with diabetes.

**1/2 cup Marukan Rice Vinegar**
**4 tsp. sugar or 2 packets of Equal Sweetener**

Mix ingredients and let sit until sweetener is dissolved.

Yield: 1/2 cup (8 servings)
One serving: 1 Tablespoon
Calories per serving: 3 with Equal, 10 with sugar
Exchanges: "free" with Equal

# Tangy Tomato Dressing

This is an inexpensive, low calorie dressing.

**1 can (8 oz.) tomato sauce***
**2 Tbl. vinegar**
**1 Tbl. Worcestershire sauce**
**1 tsp. sugar (or 1/2 pkt. Equal)**
**1 tsp. dried onion**
**1 tsp. horseradish**
**1/2 tsp. salt (optional)**
**1/4 tsp. pepper**
**2 drops Tabasco sauce**

Combine all ingredients and mix well.

Yield: 1 1/4 cups (20 servings)
One serving: 1 Tbl.
Calories per serving: 5
Exchanges: "free"
*Sodium is figured for unsalted.

# Breads & Breadings

# Applesauce Oatmeal Coffee Cake*

Applesauce adds moistness and flavor to this coffee cake. It may take longer to bake than muffins, but I prefer to make this as I'd rather pour the ingredients into one pan instead of 24 muffin tins. I also make this large amount and freeze half for another breakfast.

**3 cups oats (quick or old fashioned)**
**1 cup whole wheat flour**
**1 1/2 cups unbleached flour**
**1/2 tsp. cinnamon**
**1 tsp. allspice**
**2 tsp. baking powder**
**1 1/2 tsp. baking soda**
**1 cup firmly packed brown sugar**
**2 cup unsweetened applesauce**
**1 cup skim milk**
**6 Tbl. oil (canola)**
**1/2 cup egg substitute (equal to 2 eggs)**
**Topping:  2 Tbl.firmly packed brown sugar , 1/4 tsp. cinnamon**

Preheat oven to 375 degrees.  Combine first eight ingredients.  Mix next four ingredients and add to the dry ingredients. Stir just until moistened.  Pour into a 9-inch by 12-inch baking dish that has been sprayed with non-stick coating. Sprinkle topping ingredients over batter. Bake for 35-40 minutes or until golden brown.

Yield: 24 servings
One serving: 1 piece
Calories per serving: 170
Exchanges: 2 starch, 1/2 fat

Variations: Make half of this recipe and bake in a 9-inch by 9-inch pan for 25-30 minutes. For muffins, bake at 400 degrees for 15-20 minutes. The full recipe makes about 24 muffins.

*People with diabetes should limit use of this recipe because it contains significant amounts of sugar.

# Blueberry Coffee Cake*

This large coffee cake is great for a brunch. It also freezes well. See the variations below for a smaller coffee cake or for making muffins.

**1 cup whole wheat flour**
**1 2/3 cups unbleached flour**
**2 cups oats (quick or old fashioned)**
**1 cup firmly packed brown sugar**
**2 Tbl. baking powder**
**1 tsp. salt (optional)**
**1 tsp. cinnamon**
**1/2 tsp. ground cloves**
**2 cups skim milk**
**1/2 cup egg substitute (equal to 2 eggs)**
**6 Tbl. oil (canola)**
**2 cups fresh or frozen blueberries**
**Topping:  2 Tbl. firmly packed brown sugar, 1/4 tsp. cinnamon**

Preheat oven to 375 degrees.  Combine first eight ingredients.  Mix milk, egg, and oil.  Add to dry ingredients and mix just until moistened.  Add blueberries. Pour into a 9-inch by 12-inch baking pan that has been sprayed with non-stick coating.  Bake for 35-40 minutes or until golden brown.

Yield: 24 servings
One serving: 1 piece
Calories per serving: 160
Exchanges: 1 3/4 starch, 1/2 fat

Variations: Halve the recipe and bake in a 9-inch by 9-inch pan for 25-30 minutes.  For muffins, bake at 425 degrees for 15-20 minutes.  The full recipe makes about 24 muffins.

* People with diabetes should limit the use of this recipe because it contains significant amounts of sugar.

# Oat Bran Muffins

These muffins are very moist and are a good source of fiber. The tops don't brown well due to the low sugar content. I prefer not to use paper liners as the muffins have a tendency to stick to the paper.

**2 1/4 cups oat bran**
**1/4 cup firmly packed brown sugar**
**1 1/2 tsp. cinnamon**
**1 Tbl. baking powder**
**1 banana, mashed**
**1 small apple, grated**
**2 Tbl. dried fruit (raisins, dates, apricots)**
**1/4 cup egg substitute (equal to 1 egg)**
**1/2 cup orange juice**
**3/4 cup skim milk**
**2 tbl. oil (canola)**

Preheat oven to 425 degres. Mix first four ingredients. Set aside. Mix egg with orange juice, milk and oil. Mix fruit and blend with dry ingredients. Add liquid ingredients and mix just until moistened. Pour into muffin tins that have been sprayed with non-stick coating. Bake for 15-17 minutes.

Yield: 12 muffins
One serving: 1 muffin
Calories per serving: 115
Exchanges: 1 1/2 starch

# Refrigerator Bran Muffins*

Make this recipe to have on hand for fresh baked breakfast muffins.

**2 cups All Bran Cereal**
**2 cups boiling water**
**1 cup egg substitute (equal to 4 eggs)**
**4 cups buttermilk**
**2 1/2 cups sugar**
**1 cup oil (canola)**
**3 cups whole wheat flour**
**2 cups unbleached flour**
**5 tsp. baking soda**
**1 1/4 tsp. salt (optional)**
**2 cups dried fruit (optional)**
**4 cups Bran Buds or 100% Bran cereal**

In a small bowl, pour boiling water over the All Bran cereal and let stand until softened. In a large bowl, mix eggs, buttermilk, sugar and oil. Add the All Bran/water mixture to the egg mixture. Stir in the next four ingredients, just until moistened. If using dried fruit, add during this stage. Stir in Bran Buds or 100% Bran cereal. Batter may be covered and stored in refrigerator for up to three weeks and baked as needed.

**Conventional Oven:** Preheat oven to 375 degrees. Pour about 1/4 cup batter into muffin tins sprayed with non-stick coating or tins lined with cupcake papers. Bake for 15 minutes (20 minutes for chilled batter).

**Microwave Method:** For one muffin: Pour 1/4 cup batter into cupcake paper. Cook on high 55 to 70 seconds, rotating 1/4 turn halfway through cooking.

Yield: 56 muffins
One Serving: 1 muffin
Calories per serving: 140
Exchanges: 1 1/2 starch, 1/2 fat

*People with diabetes should limit the use of this recipe because it contains significant amounts of sugar.

# Cottage Cheese Pancakes

Try these for a quick supper.  They are excellent served with turkey sausage and the Fruit Sauce recipe in this book.

**3/4 cup egg substitute (equal to 3 eggs)**
**1/4 tsp. salt (optional)**
**1 cup low fat cottage cheese**
**1/4 cup skim milk**
**1 cup unbleached flour**
**2 Tbl. sugar or 2 to 3 pkts. of Equal sweetener**

Combine first four ingredients in blender.  Blend until smooth.  Add flour and sugar and blend again.  Spray a griddle with non-stick coating.  Cook pancakes until golden on both sides.

Yield: 12  4-inch pancakes (6 servings)
One serving: 2 pancakes
Calories per serving: 120 with Equal, 135 with sugar
Exchanges: 1 starch, 1 lean meat

# Italian Focaccia Bread

This is a great addition to many meals.  It's so easy because you start with ready made bread and add seasonings before heating.

**1 loaf (1 lb.) Focaccia bread**
**1 tsp. olive oil**
**1 tsp. Italian herb seasoning**
**1 tsp. grated Parmesan cheese**

Preheat oven to 375 degrees.  Spread olive oil over top of bread.  Sprinkle with Italian herb seasoning and cheese.  Bake for 20 minutes or until golden.

Yield: 1 loaf (about 8 servings)
One serving: 1/8 of loaf
Calories per serving: 165
Exchanges: 2 starch

# Dumplings

Add a special touch to soups and stews with this simple recipe. These are good with the Chicken Cacciatore recipe in this book.

**1 cup unbleached flour**
**1 tsp. baking powder**
**1/8 tsp. salt (optional)**
**1/3 cup skim milk**
**1/4 cup egg substitute (equal to 1 egg)**

Combine dry ingredients. Mix milk and egg substitute. Blend with dry ingredients, just until moistened. Drop by spoonfuls onto simmering liquid and follow directions below for microwave or stovetop.

**Microwave Method**: Cover and cook on high for 7 minutes, rotating 1/4 turn halfway through cooking time.

**Stovetop Method:** Cook, uncovered, for 10 minutes. Cover and cook an additional 10 minutes.

Yield: 6 dumplings (6 servings)
One serving: 1 dumpling
Calories per serving: 90
Exchanges: 1 starch

# Homemade Breading

The cornflake crumbs give a golden brown color without the addition of fat that you find in the packaged mixes. Make this large quantity to have on hand. See Nutrient Analysis to compare sodium using regular and salt-free bouillon.

**4 cups packaged cornflake crumbs**
**4 tsp. instant chicken bouillon**
**4 tsp. paprika**
**2 tsp. poultry seasoning**
**1 Tbl. Italian herb seasoning**
**1/2 tsp. pepper**
**1 tsp. garlic powder**
**1 tsp. onion powder**

Combine all ingredients and mix well. Place in an air-tight container. Mix well before using. Plan on 1/2 to 1 Tbl. of the breading for each chicken part or fish fillet.

Yield: about 4 cups
One serving: 1 Tbl.
Calories per serving: 25
Exchanges: 1/3 starch

Recipes used in:
  Oven Fried Chicken
  Oven Fried Fish
  Oven Fried Oysters
  Chicken Nuggets
  Chicken Breasts Supreme

# Gravies & Sauces

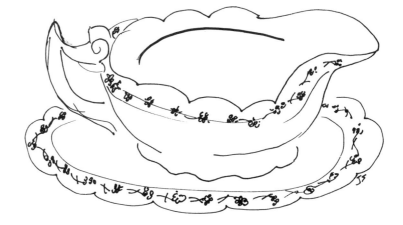

# Cornstarch Gravy

This gravy contains no fat. It is the consistency of sauces used in Chinese food and has a clearer appearance than a flour gravy. For a thicker gravy, increase cornstarch to 1 1/2 tablespoons. Canned broths have a good flavor that work well in this recipe, but be sure to remove the fat before using. Canned mushrooms (drained) can be added after the gravy thickens. See Nutrient Analysis to compare sodium using regular and salt free broth.

**1 cup cold broth, fat removed (chicken, turkey or beef)**
**1 Tbl. cornstarch**
**seasonings to taste**
**Kitchen Bouquet (optional)**

Pour 1/4 cup broth in a covered container. Add cornstarch and shake well to avoid lumps. In a small saucepan, combine remainder of broth with the cornstarch mixture. Heat on medium, stirring constantly with a wire whip, until thickened. Add a drop of Kitchen Bouquet if a darker brown color is desired.

Yield: 1 cup (8 servings)
One serving: 2 Tbl.
Calories per serving: 5
Exchanges: "free"

Note: Use 1 3/4 Tbl. cornstarch for one 14 1/2 oz. can of broth.

# Flour Gravy

This will remind you of traditional gravy but it is so much lower in calories and contains no fat. You can use canned broth or instant bouillon mixed with water. I prefer Swanson's canned broth and I remove the fat. For mushroom gravy, add one small can of drained mushrooms after the gravy is thickened. See Nutrient Analysis to compare sodium using regular or salt free broth.

**1 cup cold broth, fat removed (chicken, turkey or beef)**
**2 Tbl. flour**
**seasonings to taste**
**Kitchen Bouquet (optional)**

Pour 1/4 cup broth in a covered container. Add flour and shake well to avoid lumps. In a small saucepan, combine remainder of broth with the flour mixture. Heat on medium, stirring contantly with a wire whip, until thickened. Add a drop of Kitchen Bouquet if a darker brown color is desired.

Yield: 1 cup (8 servings)
One serving: 2 Tbl.
Calories per serving: 10
Exchanges: "free"

Note: Use 3 1/2 Tbl. of flour for one 14 1/2 oz. can of broth.

# Fresh Cucumber Sauce for Seafood

Serve this with the Oven Fried Fish or Oysters recipe in this book. It's a good replacement for tartar sauce.

**1 cup chopped cucumber (not peeled)**
**1 Tbl. lemon juice**
**1/2 cup plain nonfat yogurt**
**1/4 cup reduced calorie mayonnaise**
**1 tsp. Dijon mustard**
**1 tsp. dried onion**

Combine all ingredients. Cover and chill until serving. Serve cold with seafood.

Yield: about 1 3/4 cups (7 servings)
One serving: 1/4 cup
Calories per serving: 40
Exchanges: 1/2 vegetable, 1/2 fat

# Spanish Yogurt Sauce

Serve this with Mexican dishes in place of sour ceam.  It really tastes good!

**1 cup nonfat plain yogurt**
**1/2 tsp. dried cilantro (optional)**
**1/4 tsp. cumin**
**1 tsp. dried parsley**
**1/2 cup salsa, thick and chunky***

Mix all ingredients and refrigerate until serving.

Yield: 1 1/2 cups (6 servings)
One serving: 1/4 cup
Calories per serving: 40
Exchanges: 1 vegetable

*Sodium is figured using bottled salsa. To reduce the sodium, use the salsa recipe in this book.

Serving Suggestions:
  Serve cold with baked fish.
  Spoon over sliced tomatoes and cucumbers.

# Thick and Chunky Salsa

This recipe uses canned tomatoes and chilies so it is convenient to make anytime of the year.  Freeze in one cup portions to have on hand.  You can make this chunky or smooth, depending on your preference.  Also, choose mild to hot chiles to suit your taste. Cilantro fans will prefer to substitute fresh for the dried.

**2 cans (16 oz. each) tomatoes,\* drained**
**6 green onions, chopped**
**1-3 tsp. chopped garlic**
**1 can (4 oz.) diced green chiles**
**1 Tbl. dried cilantro (optional)**

Combine all ingredients in a blender.  Process on "chop" for 15-30 seconds, depending on desired consistency.

Yield: about 2 1/2cups (10 servings)
One serving: 1/4 cup
Calories per serving: 25
Exchanges: 1 vegetable

\*Sodium is figured for canned without salt.

# Soups & Stews

Several of these recipes make a large amount so plan on leftovers or freeze for later use. The *Cream Soup Mix* is a great low-fat substitute for canned soup in your favorite casseroles.

J. STAUER

# Cream Soup Mix

This mix is a great nonfat substitute for condensed cream soups in your favorite recipes. You can also use it as a soup and add vegetables and/or meats of your choice. Ingredients are listed for the equivalent of eight cans and for one can. Make the larger amount and store it in an air tight container. Stir well before using. See Nutrient Analysis of Recipes to compare sodium using regular or salt free bouillon.

| Equivalent to 8 Cans | Equivalent to 1 can |
|---|---|
| 2 cups nonfat dry milk | 1/4 cup nonfat dry milk |
| 3/4 cup cornstarch | 1 1/2 Tbl. cornstarch |
| 2 Tbl. dried onion | 3/4 tsp. dried onion |
| 1/2 tsp. pepper | dash pepper |
| 1 tsp. dried basil | 1/8 tsp. dried basil |
| 1 tsp. dried thyme | 1/8 tsp. dried thyme |
| 1/4 cup instant chicken bouillon | 1/2 Tbl. instant bouillon |

Combine all ingredients and mix well. Use in recipes in place of condensed cream of chicken soup (be sure to follow directions below to reconstitute). Add mushrooms to substitute for condensed cream of mushroom soup.

**Methods for making the equivalent of one can of condensed soup:**

**Stovetop Method**: In saucepan, combine 1/3 cup dry mix with 1 1/4 cups cold water. Stir over low heat until thickened.

**Microwave Method**: In a glass measuring cup, combine 1/3 cup dry soup mix with 1 1/4 cups cold water. Heat on high for 4-5 minutes, stirring several times, until mixture thickens.

Yield: 2 2/3 cups dry mix (equivalent to 8 cans of condensed soup)
One serving: 1/3 cup dry mix (equivalent to one can of soup)
Calories per 1/3 cup, dry mix: 175
Exchanges: 1 starch, 1 milk

Recipes used in:
  Mexican Chicken Casserole
  Beef, Cabbage, and Noodles
  Clam Chowder, Cream of Mushroom Soup, Cream of Vegetable Soup

# Clam Chowder

This can be a quick meal, using foods that you usually have available. Add a hot roll and sliced fruit to complete a light supper.

1/3 cup Cream Soup Mix (page 70)
water
1 cup skim milk
1/4 cup diced green pepper
3/4 cup diced potato
1 can (6.5 oz.) minced clams

**Stovetop Method:** Drain liquid from clams into measuring cup and add water to equal 1 1/4 cups. Cook green pepper and potato in this liquid until tender. Meanwhile, in a saucepan, combine 1/3 cup dry soup mix with milk. Cook over low heat, stirring constantly to avoid scorching, until thickened. Add vegetables (including liquid) and minced clams. Heat thoroughly.

**Microwave Method:** Cook potatoes and green pepper (covered), on high, for 3 minutes, stirring halfway through cooking time. Set aside. Drain liquid from clams into a four-cup glass measuring cup. Add water to equal 1 1/4 cups. Add 1/3 cup dry soup mix and heat on high for 4-5 minutes, stirring several times, until mixture thickens. Add milk, vegetables, and clams. Cook on high for 2-3 minutes (stirring halfway) until heated throughly.

Yield: about 3 cups (3 servings)
One serving: 1 cup
Calories per serving:165
Exchanges: 1 milk, 1/2 lean meat, 1/2 starch

# Cream of Mushroom Soup

Serve this for lunch on a cold winter day.  If fresh mushrooms aren't handy, use canned.  You can also substitute onion for the green pepper.

**1/3 cup Cream Soup Mix (page 70)**
**1 1/4 cups water**
**1 cup skim milk**
**3/4 cup sliced mushrooms (or 1/2 cup canned)**
**1/4 cup diced green pepper**

**Stovetop Method:** Combine vegetables and water in a saucepan.  Cover and cook until tender. Set aside. In a saucepan, combine 1/3 cup dry mix with 1 cup cold milk.  Cook over low heat, stirring constantly to avoid scorching, until thickened.  Add vegetables and the water they were cooked in.  Heat thoroughly.

**Microwave Method:** Cook vegetables (covered), on high, for 2 minutes, stirring halfway through cooking time.  Set aside.  In a four-cup glass measuring cup, combine 1/3 cup dry soup mix with 1 1/4 cups cold water.  Heat on high for 4-5 minutes, stirring several times, until mixture thickens.  Add milk and vegetables.  Cook on high for 1-2 minutes until thoroughly heated.

Yield: about 3 cups (3 servings)
One serving: 1 cup
Calories per serving: 95
Exchanges: 1 milk

# Cream of Vegetable Soup

This is a great way to use up leftover vegetables. See the variations below for other ingredients.

**1/3 cup Cream Soup Mix (page 70)**
**1 1/4 cups water**
**1 cup skim milk**
**1 cup chopped vegetables (fresh, frozen or canned)**

**Stovetop Method:** Combine vegetables and 1 1/4 cups of water in a saucepan. Cover and cook until vegetables are tender. Set aside. Combine 1/3 cup dry mix with 1 cup cold milk. Cook over low heat, stirring constantly to avoid scorching, until thickened. Add vegetables and the water they were cooked in. Heat thoroughly.

**Microwave Method:** Cook vegetables (covered), on high, for 2-3 minutes, stirring halfway through cooking time. Set aside. In a four-cup glass measuring cup, combine 1/3 cup dry soup mix with 1 1/4 cups cold water. Heat on high for 4-5 minutes, stirring several times, until mixture thickens. Add milk and vegetables. Cook for 1-2 minutes until thoroughly heated.

Yield: about 3 cups (3 servings)
One serving: 1 cup
Calories per serving: 95
Exchanges: 1 milk

Variations:
   Add cooked, diced chicken or seafood.
   Add cooked noodles or rice.

# Chili Con Carne

This is a great dish for a party because it really makes a large amout and it tastes so good.  I also recommend freezing leftovers in one cup containers to have handy for lunch.

3 cans (15 oz. each) kidney beans, drained
2 large onions, chopped
2 green pepper, chopped
2 lbs. extra lean ground beef (9% fat or less) or turkey (7% fat)
2 cans (16 oz. each) tomatoes*
2 cans (8 oz. each) tomato sauce*
1/4 tsp. paprika
2 bay leaves, crumbled
2 Tbl. chili powder

Spray a large kettle with non-stick cooking spray and brown the meat.  Add remaining ingredients.  Cover and simmer for 1 hour.

Yield: about 3 quarts (12 servings)
One serving: 1 cup
Calories per serving: turkey-230; beef-250
Exchanges: 2 medium fat meat, 2 vegetable, 1/2 starch

*Sodium is figured for canned without salt.

# Chilled Tomato-Shrimp Soup

You can make this with canned or frozen shrimp (thaw first).  It's great for a quick lunch.

**1 cup tomato juice***
**1/2 cup cooked shrimp**
**1/2 Tbl. lemon juice**
**1/8 tsp. Worcestershire sauce**
**1/2 tsp. prepared horseradish**
**1 drop Tabasco sauce**

Combine ingredients.  Chill before serving.

Yield: about 1 1/4  cups (1 servings)
One serving: 1 1/4 cups
Calories per serving: 110
Exchanges**:  2 lean meat, 2 vegetable

*Sodium is figured for unsalted.

**Due to the low fat content of shrimp, the calories are less than the exchanges would compute.

# Fish Stew

This quick dish combines vegetables with fish.  Serve with French bread to complete the meal.

**1 1/2 tsp. instant beef bouillon**
**1 1/2 cups water**
**1 tsp. chopped garlic**
**1 Tbl. catsup**
**1 onion, sliced**
**1 cup sliced carrots**
**1 can (16 oz.)  green beens,\* drained**
**1 lb. fish fillets**
**1/2 tsp. dried basil**

**Microwave Method:** In a microwave safe dish, combine bouillon, water, garlic, and catsup. Add vegetables and top with fish and basil. Cover with plastic wrap (vent one corner).  Heat 10 minutes on high, rotating 1/4 turn halfway through cooking time.  Fish is done when it flakes easily.

**Stovetop Method:** In a skillet, combine bouillon, water, garlic, and catsup.  Add vegetables and top with fish and basil. Bring to a boil. Reduce heat and simmer, covered, for 10 minutes or until fish flakes easily with a fork.

Yield: 4 servings (about 6 cups)
One serving: 1/4 recipe
Calories per serving: 170
Exchanges\*\*: 3 lean meat, 2 vegetable

\*Sodium is figured using canned without salt.

\*\*Due to the low fat content of fish, the calories are less than the exchanges would compute.

# Italian Cioppino

I like the flavor of this seafood stew. Don't limit yourself to just using fish since shrimp, clams and crab also taste good in this dish.

**1 lb. fish fillets**
**1 cup chopped onion**
**2 tsp. chopped garlic**
**1 can (8 oz.) tomato sauce\***
**1 can (28 oz.) tomatoes,\* cut up**
**1 bay leaf**
**1 tsp. each: dried basil, dried thyme, dried marjoram, and dried oregano**
**1/4 tsp. pepper**
**1 Tbl. dried parsley flakes**
**1/2 cup white wine or chicken broth**

Mix all ingredients listed, except fish, in a saucepan. Simmer for 20 to 30 minutes, stirring occasionally. Meanwhile, cut fish into 1/2 inch chunks. Add fish and cook 10 minutes or until done.

Yield: about 6 cups (4 servings)
One serving: 1 1/2 cups
Calories per serving: 215
Exchanges\*\*: 3 lean meat, 3 vegetable

Variations: Use a combination of seafoods such as shrimp, clams, and crab. If uncooked, add with the fish. If using precooked seafood, just add to heat. Add 2 cups sliced zucchini before simmering.

\*Sodium is figured for canned without salt.

\*\*Due to the low fat content of fish, the calories are less than the exchanges would compute.

# New England Fish Chowder

This low calorie version of chowder has an excellent flavor.

**1/2 cup chopped onion**
**1/2 tsp. dried thyme**
**1 1/2 cups diced potato**
**1/2 cup chopped green pepper**
**1 cup water**
**3/4 lb. fish fillets, cut into 1-inch pieces**
**1/4 lb. scallops**
**2 cups skim milk**
**2 Tbl. cornstarch**
**1/2 tsp. salt (optional)**
**1/8 tsp. pepper**

In a medium saucepan, combine first five ingredients and bring to a boil. Reduce heat to low and simmer, covered, for 15 minutes or until potatoes are tender. Add fish and scallops. Cook, covered, for 8 minutes. Mix cornstarch with milk and remaining ingredients. Stir into soup and simmer, stirring occasionally, until seafood is cooked and soup is slightly thickened.

Yield: about 6 cups (6 servings)
One serving: 1 cup
Calories per serving: 150
Exchanges*: 2 lean meat, 1 starch

*Due to the low fat content of fish, the calories are less than the exchanges would compute.

# French Onion Soup

This is good on a cold winter day. See Nutrient Analysis of Recipes to compare sodium using regular or salt free broth.

**1 1/2 cups thinly sliced onions**
**6 cups beef broth**
**1/4 tsp. pepper**
**3 oz. grated, part skim mozzarella cheese**
**6 slices French bread, toasted**

Mix first three ingredients and simmer for 20 minutes. Divide soup into 6 ovenproof bowls. Top each with a slice of toasted French bread and 1/2 ounce of cheese. Broil until cheese is melted.

Yield: 6 servings
One serving: 1 bowl
Calories per serving: 135
Exchanges: 1 starch, 1/2 medium fat meat, 1/2 vegetable

# Minestrone Soup

Don't shy away from this recipe because of the long list of ingredients. It's really quick to put together, but allow 1 1/2 hours for cooking. You'll have enough for more than one meal so plan on freezing for later. See Nutrient Analysis of Recipes to compare sodium using regular or salt free broth.

**1/3 cup each: dried green split peas, dried lentils, and pearl barley**
**1/2 cup dried black-eyed peas**
**3 1/2 cups fat free beef broth**
**4 1/2 cups water**
**1 can (16 oz.) tomatoes,\* undrained**
**2 1/2 cups chopped vegetables of your choice:**
**    celery, onion, zucchini, carrots, green pepper, mushrooms, etc.**
**2 tsp. dried basil**
**1 1/2 tsp. dried oregano**
**1 tsp. salt (optional)**
**1/2 tsp. pepper**
**1 tsp. chopped garlic**
**2 bay leaves**
**3 1/3 Tbl. Parmesan cheese**

Wash peas, lentils and barley. Mix with broth and water in a large kettle. Bring to a boil. Cover, reduce heat, and simmer for 30 minutes. Add remaining ingredients and simmer another hour or until peas are tender. Discard bay leaves. Serve sprinkled with Parmesan cheese.

Yield: about 2 1/2 quarts (10 servings)
One serving: 1 cup soup and 1 tsp. Parmesan cheese
Calories per serving: 120
Exchanges: 1 starch, 1 1/2 vegetable

\*Sodium is figured for canned without salt.

# Oriental Noodle Soup

This is a light soup with a good flavor. I especially like the fineness of the angel hair pasta in this recipe. See Nutrient Analysis of Recipes to compare sodium using Swanson's broth with 30% less salt, and for salt free broth.

**3 cans (14 1/2 oz. each) Swanson's chicken broth (30% less salt)**
**3/4 tsp. garlic powder**
**1/4 tsp. pepper**
**3 oz. angel hair pasta**
**4 green onions, sliced thin**
**3/4 cup thinly sliced mushrooms**
**1/2 cup thinly sliced carrot**

Remove fat from soup. Combine first three ingredients in a stockpot. Bring to a boil. Add pasta and cook for 1 minute. Add vegetables and cook an additional 2 minutes.

Yield: about 5 1/2 cups (5 1/2 servings)
One serving: 1 cup
Calories per serving: 80
Exchanges: 1/2 vegetable, 3/4 starch

# Taco Soup

This makes a large amount so plan on freezing for another meal or invite friends over. This can be served with a dollop of nonfat yogurt. If you like spicy food, use a whole package of taco seasoning.

**1 lb. extra lean ground beef (9% fat or less) or ground turkey (7% fat)**
**1  medium onion, chopped**
**1 can (16 oz.) tomato sauce***
**2 cans (16 oz. each) tomatoes***
**2 cans (16 oz. each) pinto or chili beans, undrained**
**1/2  pkg. taco seasoning**

Brown meat with onion in a stockpot that has been sprayed with non-stick coating. Add remaining ingredients and simmer for 30 minutes.

Yield: 2 1/2 quarts (10 servings)
One serving: 1 cup
Calories per serving: turkey-150; beef-160
Exchanges: 1 medium fat meat, 1 1/2  vegetable, 1/2 starch

*Sodium is figured for canned without salt.

# Three Bean Soup

This can be cooked in less than 30 minutes since almost every ingredient is canned.  You can omit the fresh vegetables or substitute others of your choice.

**1 1/2 tsp. chopped garlic**
**1 can (28 oz.)  tomatoes,* cut up**
**1 cup water**
**1 can (6 oz.) tomato paste**
**1 tsp. chili powder**
**1 Tbl. Dijon mustard**
**1 tsp. dried basil**
**1 tsp. dried oregano**
**1/2 tsp. ground cumin**
**1/2 tsp. pepper**
**1 can (15 oz.) kidney beans, drained**
**1 can (15 oz.) black eyed peas, drained**
**1 can (15 oz.) garbanzo beans, drained**
**1 can (15 oz.) whole kernel corn, drained**
**1 cup chopped carrots**
**1 cup chopped zucchini or celery**
**1 medium onion, chopped**

Combine first 13 ingredients.  Bring to a boil.  Reduce heat and simmer, covered, for 10 minutes.  Stir in vegetables and simmer, covered, for 10 minutes more.

Yield: about 3 quarts (12 servings)
One serving: 1 cup
Calories per serving: 125
Exchanges: 1 starch, 2 vegetable

Variation: Top each bowl with 1 tsp. of Parmesan cheese.

*Sodium is figured for canned without salt.

# Zero Vegetable Soup

You can use fresh, canned, or frozen vegetables in this soup. Fresh shredded cabbage tastes especially good. See Nutrient Analysis of Recipes to compare sodium using Swanson's broth with 30% less salt and for salt free broth.

**1 can (14 1/2 oz.) Swanson's chicken broth (30% less salt)**
**1 1/2 cups sliced vegetables, any combination of:**
   **cabbage**
   **broccoli**
   **carrots**
   **onions**
   **zucchini**
   **celery**
   **tomatoes**
   **cauliflower**
   **mushrooms**

**Stovetop Method:** Skim fat off of broth. Add vegetables. Cover and simmer for 10-15 minutes or until vegetables are done.

**Microwave Method:** Skim fat off of broth. Add vegetables. Cover and cook on high for approximately 5-10 minutes, stirring twice.

Yield: about 2 1/2 cups (2 servings)
One serving: 1 1/4 cups
Calories per serving: 45
Exchanges: 2 vegetable

Variation: Add bite size pieces of meat or seafood at the end of cooking time and heat thoroughly.

# Vegetables

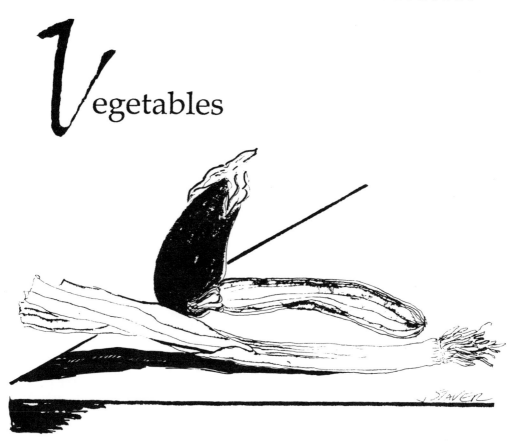

It is hard to beat the good taste of plain vegetables cooked in the microwave or steamed just until crisp. For that reason you will not find a lot of recipes in this section. Consult your microwave cookbook for a table of cooking times. Also, for more vegetable ideas see the section on *Salads*.

# Basil Tomatoes

The addition of basil gives an excellent flavor to fresh tomatoes.

**2 large tomatoes, diced or sliced (about 2 cups)**
**1 tsp. dried basil**
**1 tsp. chopped garlic**
**1/2 tsp. salt (optional)**
**1/8 Tsp. pepper**

Mix ingredients and let sit at room temperature at least one hour.  Serve plain or on a lettuce leaf.

Yield: 2 cups (4 servings)
One serving: 1/2 cup
Calories per serving: 15
Exchanges: 1 vegetable

# Italian Herb Tomatoes

Herbs and vinegar give us another good way to serve fresh tomatoes.

**2 cups tomatoes, sliced**
**1/4 cup red wine vinegar**
**1/4 tsp. Italian herb seasoning**
**1/8 tsp. pepper**
**1/8 tsp. garlic powder**

Arrange tomatoes in a shallow bowl. Mix remaining ingredients and pour over tomatoes.  Marinate 1/2 - 4 hours before serving.

Yield: about 2 cups (4 servings)
One serving: 1/2 cup
Calories per serving: 20
Exchanges: 1 vegetable

# Gourmet Cucumbers

This is a family favorite!  The seasoned dressing gives the cucumbers a great flavor.

**1 cucumber, thinly sliced (not peeled)**
**1/2 cup sliced onion (Walla Walla onions are best)**
**1/3 cup Marukan Seasoned Gourmet Rice Vinegar Lite Dressing**
  *or Salt-Free Sweetened Rice Vinegar (page 54)*
**1/4 tsp. pepper**

Mix all ingredients.  Serve immediately or let stand in refrigerator for 2 or 3 hours.  Serve with slotted spoon or drain liquid before serving.

Yield: about 2 cups (4 servings)
One serving: 1/2 cup
Calories per serving: 25
Exchanges: 1 vegetable

# Marinated Vegetables

You'll find this a good substitute for a salad.  This recipe can be prepared in advance and refrigerated for several days.

**4 cups water**
**4 cups vegetables, cut into bite size pieces, such as: broccoli, celery, green**
  **pepper, carrots, mushrooms, cauliflower, green beans, frozen or fresh**
  **brussel sprouts**
**1/4 cup low calorie Italian dressing**

Bring water to a boil.  Add vegetables and return to a boil. Drain immediately. Mix vegetables with Italian dressing and marinate in refrigerator for one hour or until well chilled.  Drain before serving.

Yield: about 4 cups (8 servings)
One serving: 1/2 cup
Calories per serving: 25
Exchanges: 1 vegetable

# Mexican Vegetables

Serve this as a cold side dish with Mexican food.  It adds color and has a great flavor.

**1 cup chopped cucumber (with peel)**
**1 can (8 3/4 oz.) corn,\* drained**
**1 can (16 oz.) stewed tomatoes\***
**2 Tbl. chopped red pepper**
**2 Tbl. chopped green pepper**
**2 Tbl. red wine vinegar**
**1/2 tsp. garlic**
**1/2 tsp. cumin**
**1/4 tsp. dried cilantro**
**1/4 tsp. salt (optional)**
**1/8 tsp. ground pepper**

Combine ingredients and mix well.  Serve cold.

Yield: about 3 1/2 cups (7 servings)
One serving: 1/2 cup
Calories per serving: 35
Exchanges: 1 vegetable

\*Sodium is figured for canned without salt.

# Seasoned Green Beans

This dish can be served either hot or cold. The seasoned vinegar and bacon bits really add a good flavor to the beans.

**1 Tbl. Marukan Seasoned Gourmet Rice Vinegar Lite Dressing**
  *or Salt-Free Sweetened Rice Vinegar (page 54)*
**1 Tbl. dried onion**
**1 Tbl. water**
**1/4 tsp. pepper**
**1 can (16 oz.) green beans,\* drained**
**2 tsp. bacon flavored soy bits**

Place water in bowl with dried onion and let sit for 5-10 minutes. Add remaining ingredients and mix well. Serve hot or cold.

Yield: about 2 cups (4 servings)
One serving: 1/2 cup
Calories per serving: 30
Exchanges: 1 vegetable

*Sodium is figured for canned without salt.

# Zucchini, Tomato and Onion

I like to prepare this dish in the summer when I'm looking for ways to use tomatoes and zucchini.

**2 cups sliced onion**
**2 cups sliced tomato**
**2 cups sliced zucchini**
**1 1/2 tsp. Italian herb seasoning**
**1/2 tsp. salt (optional)**
**dash of pepper**

Preheat oven to 350 degrees. Layer onion, tomato, and zucchini in a 2 qt. casserole dish that has been sprayed with a non-stick coating. Sprinkle each layer with seasonings. Bake for 30-45 minutes, depending on how soft you want the vegetables.

Yield: about 3 1/2 cups (7 servings)
One serving: 1/2 cup
Calories per serving: 35
Exchanges: 1 vegetable

# Refried beans

Try this low fat version of refried beans. These are made without the addition of fat which is a common ingredient in the traditional recipe.

**1 can (15 1/4 oz.) pinto beans, drained**
**1/2 cup salsa**

Drain beans. Spray pan with non-stick coating. Add beans and mash. Add salsa and heat thoroughly.

Yield: 4 servings
One serving: 1/4 recipe
Calories per serving: 65
Exchanges: 1 starch

# Ranch Beans

Try this "dressed up" version of baked beans. It can be served as a side dish or as a main dish.

**1/4 cup chopped green pepper**
**1 can (16 oz.) vegetarian baked beans**
**1 can (15 oz.) red kidney beans, drained**
**2 Tbl. catsup**
**2 Tbl. molasses**
**1 Tbl. Dijon mustard**
**1/2 tsp. dried onion**

**Stovetop Method:** Place all ingredients in saucepan and heat thoroughly (about 10 minutes).

**Microwave Method:** Place all ingredients in a microwave safe bowl. Cover with wax paper, cook on high for 5 minutes, stirring halfway through cooking time.

Yield: about 3 cups (6 servings)
One serving size: 1/2 cup
Calories per serving: 150
Exchanges: 2 starch

# $S$alads

Salad making can be quick if you buy pre-washed and cut vegetables. They are available in grocery stores and deli's. Using a food processor also saves time, especially if you chop foods for several recipes at once. Several of the salads included in this section can be served as main dishes and a few are also good sandwich spreads.

# Apple Salad Mold

This is a refreshing salad that goes well with many dishes.

**1 pkg. (0.3 oz.) sugar-free cherry Jello***
**1 cup boiling water**
**1/2 cup apple juice**
**1/2 cup cold water**
**1 medium unpeeled apple, chopped (about 1 1/2 cups)**
**1/2 cup chopped celery**

Dissolve Jello in boiling water. Combine juice and water. Add to Jello and stir. Refrigerate until slightly thickened. Add apple and celery. Mix well. Refrigerate until set.

Yield: about 2 1/2 cups (5 servings)
One serving: 1/2 cup
Calories per serving: 35
Exchanges: 1/2 fruit

*Any flavor of Jello may be substututed.

# Fruit Salad

This is so easy to put together. You can make it different each time by varying the fruit and the flavor of the yogurt.

**4 cups, sliced fruit**
**1 cup fruit flavored nonfat yogurt (sweetened with NutraSweet)**

Mix fruit with yogurt in a serving bowl.

Yield: 4 cups (8 servings)
One serving: 1/2 cup
Calories per serving: 55
Exchanges: 1 fruit

# Cabbage Salad

To save time, use a food processor to chop the cabbage. Also, use the processor to prepare vegetables for the next few days.

**6 cups chopped cabbage**
**3 green onions, chopped**
**3 Tbl. sesame seeds**

**Dressing:**
**3 Tbl. Marukan Seasoned Gourmet Rice Vinegar Lite Dressing**
  *or Salt-Free Sweetened Rice Vinegar (page 54)*

Mix first three ingredients. Add rice vinegar and mix well. Let stand for several hours in the refrigerator.

Yield: about 6 cups (6 servings)
One serving: 1 cup
Calories per serving: 55
Exchanges: 2 vegetable

Variations: Just before serving, add cooked, cubed chicken or shrimp.

# Shrimp Coleslaw

Try this colorful coleslaw. It's low in fat because nonfat yogurt is used for part of the dressing. Fresh or imitation crab can be substituted for the shrimp.

**1 medium head of cabbage, shredded (5 cups)**
**1 small green pepper, diced**
**1 carrot, chopped**
**2 green onions, chopped**
**2 cups cooked shrimp (frozen works well)**

**Dressing:**
**1 cup nonfat plain yogurt**
**2 tsp. dried dill**
**3 Tbl. Marukan Seasoned Gourmet Rice Vinegar Lite Dressing**
  *or Salt-Free Sweetened Rice Vinegar (page 54)*
**1/2 tsp. pepper**
**1/2 tsp. celery seed**
**1/2 tsp. Dijon style mustard**

In a large bowl, combine all vegetables with shrimp. Mix dressing ingredients and pour over vegetables. Serve immediately or chill for one hour before serving.

Yield: about 8 cups (8 servings)
One serving: 1 cup
Calories per serving: 75
Exchanges: 1 lean meat, 1 vegetable

# Broccoli Salad

Make the amount listed and you'll probably have enough for leftovers.  If you prefer the crunch of the soy bacon bits, add them just before serving.

**4 cups broccoli flowerets**
**4 tsp. bacon flavor soy bits**
**2 tomatoes, chopped**
**1 cup sliced mushrooms**

**Dressing:**
**2 tsp. Parsley Patch Salt Free Seasoning**
**4 Tbl. reduced calorie mayonnaise**

Mix vegetables and bacon bits in a bowl.  Mix seasoning with mayonnaise.  Add dressing to vegetables and mix well.

Yield: about 6 cups (6 servings)
One serving: 1 cup
Calories per serving: 70
Exchanges: 1 fat, 1 vegetable

# Fiesta Vegetable Salad

This colorful salad is a good choice for a potluck.  Use a food processor to save time chopping the vegetables.

**1 box (0.3 oz.) sugar-free lime Jello**
**1 cup boiling water**
**1/3 cup reduced calorie mayonnaise**
**3/4 cup skim milk**
**1/2 tsp. salt (optional)**
**1 tsp. prepared horseradish**
**1 Tbl. vinegar**
**1/2 cup grated or chopped celery**
**1/2 cup grated or chopped cabbage**
**1/2 cup grated or chopped carrots**
**2 Tbl. chopped green pepper**
**2 Tbl. chopped pimento**

Dissolve Jello in boiling water, add mayonnaise and stir with wire whip until mayonnaise is dissolved.  Add remaining ingredients.  Mix well.  Refrigerate until set, about 2 to 3 hours.

Yield: about 3 cups (6 servings)
One serving: 1/2 cup
Calories per serving: 80
Exchanges: 1 vegetable, 1 fat

# Greek Salad

The red and yellow peppers give this salad an especially good flavor.  It tastes best when marinated for several hours and is great the next day.

**1 green pepper, sliced**
**1 red pepper, sliced**
**1 yellow pepper, sliced**
**1 unpeeled cucumber, sliced**
**2 Tbl. lemon juice**
**3 Tbl. red wine vinegar**
**1/4 tsp. dried oregano**
**1/2 brick (4 oz.) feta cheese**

Mix peppers and cucumber in a bowl.  Add lemon juice, vinegar, and oregano.  Mix well.  Cover and marinate.  Toss well before serving and top with crumbled feta cheese.

Yield: about 8 cups (8 servings)
One serving: 1 cup
Calories per serving: 50
Exchanges: 1 vegetable, 1/3 medium fat meat

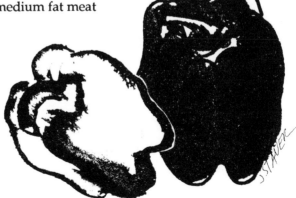

# Three Bean Salad

Keep these canned beans on hand so you can put together a salad in a matter of minutes.

**1 can (16 oz.) green beans,\* drained**
**1 can (8 oz.) garbanzo beans,\* drained**
**1 can (8 oz.) kidney beans, drained**
**1/4 cup Marukan Seasoned Gourmet Rice Vinegar Lite Dressing**
  *or Salt-Free Sweetened Rice Vinegar (page 54)*
**2 tsp. Parsley Patch Salt Free Seasoning**
**1 Tbl. dried onion soaked in 1 Tbl. water**

Combine beans in a large bowl. Add remaining ingredients and mix well. Drain before serving.

Yield: about 3 cups (6 servings)
One serving: 1/2 cup
Calories per serving: 95
Exchanges: 1 starch, 1/2 vegetable

\*Sodium is figured for canned without salt.

# Vegetable Bean Salad

This variation of the three bean salad uses fresh vegetables in place of some of the beans.

**1 can (8 oz.) green beans\* or garbanzo beans, drained**
**1 can (8 oz.) kidney beans, drained**
**1/2 cup sliced carrots**
**1/2 cup bite-size pieces of cauliflower**
**1/2 cup bite-size pieces of broccoli**
**1/4 cup Marukan Seasoned Gourmet Rice Vinegar Lite Dressing**
  *or Salt-Free Sweetened Rice Vinegar (page 54)*
**2 tsp. Parsley Patch Salt Free Seasoning**
**1 Tbl. dried onion soaked in 1 Tbl. water**

Combine vegetables in a bowl. Mix vinegar with seasoning. Add to vegetables and mix well. Drain before serving.

Yield: about 3 cups (6 servings)
One serving: 1/2 cup
Calories per serving: 60
Exchanges: 1/2 starch, 1 vegetable

\*Sodium is figured for canned without salt.

# Herb Potato Salad

The mustard and seasonings make this a tasty potato salad.  Try using new red potatoes for added color.

**1 lb. potatoes (about 4 cups)**
**1/2 cup sliced radishes (optional)**

**Dressing:**
**3 Tbl. nonfat plain yogurt**
**1 Tbl. reduced calorie mayonnaise**
**1 1/2 tsp. Dijon mustard**
**1/2 tsp. chopped garlic**
**1/2 tsp. dried basil**
**1/4 tsp. dried thyme**
**1/4 tsp. onion powder**
**1/4 tsp. salt (optional)**

Scrub potatoes and cube.  Place in medium saucepan and cover with water. Bring to a boil.  Cover, reduce heat and simmer 12 minutes or until potatoes are done.  Drain.  Mix dressing ingredients.  Combine hot potatoes, dressing and radishes.  Serve hot or cold.

Yield: 6 servings
One serving: 1/6 recipe
Calories per serving: 80
Exchanges: 1 starch

# Lentil Rice Salad

You'll like the combination of vegetables and grains in this dish. This recipe makes a large amount.

1/2 cup lentils, washed
1 1/2 cups water
1 cup chopped tomato
1/4 cup sliced green onion
1 cup diced carrots
3/4 cup chopped green pepper
1 1/2 cups broccoli flowerets
1 Tbl. dried parsley
3/4 cup quick cooking brown rice

Dressing:
3 Tbl. Marukan Seasoned Gourmet Rice Vinegar Lite Dressing
  *or Salt-Free Sweetened Rice Vinegar (page 54)*
1 Tbl. lemon juice
1 1/2 tsp. Dijon mustard

Add lentils to water in a medium saucepan and bring to a boil. Reduce heat, cover, and simmer for 20 minutes. Drain. Cook rice according to package directions. Prepare vegetables while lentils are cooking. Mix lentils, rice, and vegetables. Mix dressing ingredients and pour over vegetable mixture. Chill well before serving.

Yield: 7 cups ( 7 servings)
One serving: 1 cup
Calories per serving: 115
Exchanges: 1 starch, 1 1/2 vegetable

# Macaroni Salad

The red pepper adds color to this dish while the rice vinegar and mustard add a special flavor.

**8 oz. uncooked elbow macaroni**
**2 cups sliced celery**
**2 cups sliced red pepper**
**1/4 cup chopped onion (optional)**

**Dressing:**
**1/2 cup reduced calorie mayonnaise**
**1 Tbl. Dijon mustard**
**1/3 cup Marukan Seasoned Gourmet Rice Vinegar Lite Dressing**
   *or Salt-Free Sweetened Rice Vinegar (page 54)*
**1/4 tsp. pepper**

Cook macaroni according to package directions. Drain and cool. Prepare vegetables and set aside. Mix dressing ingredients until smooth. Mix macaroni, vegetables, and dressing.

Yield: about 8 cups (8 servings)
One serving: 1 cup
Calories per serving: 175
Exchanges: 1 1/4 starch, 1 fat, 1 vegetable

# Oriental Rice and Seafood Salad

This is a delicious recipe that makes enough for a crowd. I really like the flavor you get from the soy sauce and rice vinegar. See variations below for more ways to serve this recipe.

**2 cups cooked brown rice (use quick cooking)**
**1 can (16 oz.) bean sprouts, drained**
**2 stalks celery, diagonally sliced**
**1/4 cup chopped green pepper**
**2 green onions, thinly sliced**
**1 lb. cooked shrimp (frozen works well)**
**1 can (8 oz.) sliced water chestnuts, drained**
**1/4 cup Marukan Seasoned Gourmet Rice Vinegar Lite Dressing**
   *or Salt-Free Sweetened Rice Vinegar (page 54)*
**2 Tbl. soy sauce**

Combine first seven ingredients. Mix vinegar and soy sauce. Pour over salad and mix well. Chill before serving.

Yield: about 8 cups (8 servings)
One serving: 1 cup
Calories per serving: 140
Exchanges*: 1 vegetable, 1 1/2 lean meat, 3/4 starch

Variations: Substitute crab or chicken for shrimp.
This may also be served as a rice salad without the addition of seafood or meat.

*Due to the low fat content of shrimp, the calories are less than the exchanges would compute.

# Curry Tuna Salad

Try this for a different tuna salad. The taste of curry and the crunch of water chestnuts make this especially good.

**1 tsp. dried onion**
**1 Tbl. lemon juice**
**2 cans (6 1/2 oz. each) water pack tuna, drained**
**1 can (8 oz.) sliced water chestnuts, drained**
**1/4 cup reduced calorie mayonnaise**
**2 tsp. soy sauce**
**1 tsp. curry**

Mix onion with lemon juice. Set aside. Mix tuna and chestnuts. Make dressing with mayonnaise, onion, lemon juice, soy sauce and curry. Mix with tuna and chestnuts.

Yield: about 3 cups (4 servings)
One serving: 3/4 cup
Calories per serving: 180
Exchanges: 3 lean meat, 1/2 vegetable

Serving suggestions:
   Serve on a bed of lettuce.
   Spread 1/2 cup on a toasted English muffin half and heat under broiler until hot.

# Seafood Salad

This recipe is good on lettuce or as a sandwich spread. Substituting shrimp for part, or all, of the crab also tastes good. Sodium can be significantly reduced by using fresh crab instead of the imitation.

**1 lb. imitation crab**
**1/4 cup chopped green onion**
**1 cup chopped celery**
**2 Tbl. reduced calorie mayonnaise**
**2 Tbl. nonfat yogurt**
**1 oz. grated, low fat cheddar cheese**
**1/4 tsp. paprika**
**1 Tbl. lemon juice**

Combine all ingredients and mix well.

Yield: about 4 cups (8 servings)
One serving: 1/2 cup
Calories per serving: 90
Exchanges: 1 lean meat, 1 vegetable

Serving Suggestion:
    Serve 1/2 cup on a toasted English muffin half and broil until cheese is melted.

# Chicken and Fruit Salad

If you like fruit salad, you'll like this combination with chicken. When straw-berries are not in season, substitute another fresh fruit.

**Dressing:**
**1/3 cup nonfat strawberry yogurt (sweetened with NutraSweet)**
**1 Tbl. reduced calorie mayonnaise**
**1 Tbl. orange juice**

**2 cups cooked and cubed chicken or turkey**
**1 cup strawberries, halved**
**1 small banana, sliced**
**2  oranges, peeled and cut into chunks**
**1/2 cup sliced celery**
**1 1/2 cups seedless grapes**
**lettuce leaves**

Mix first three ingredients for dressing. Combine remaining ingredients (except lettuce) and mix well with dressing. Serve on lettuce leaves.

Yield: about 7 1/2 cups (5 servings)
One serving: 1 1/2 cups
Calories per serving: 200
Exchanges: 1 1/2 fruit, 2 lean meat

# Chicken and Spinach Salad

This is a great summer meal.  The combination of fruits with the spinach and chicken is really good.  Substitute other fresh fruit in season when fresh strawberries are not available.

**6 oz. spinach, fresh**
**2 oranges, peeled and cut into chunks**
**2 cups cooked and cubed chicken**
**2 cups strawberries**

**Dressing:**
**3 Tbl. red wine vinegar**
**3 Tbl. orange juice**
**1 1/2 Tbl. oil (canola)**
**1/4 tsp. dry mustard**
**1/3 tsp. poppy seeds**

Mix dressing ingredients and refrigerate.  Wash spinach and tear into bite size pieces.  Add oranges, chicken and strawberries.  Serve with dressing.

Yield: about 14 cups (7 servings)
One serving: 2 cups
Calories per serving: 135
Exchanges: 1 1/2 lean meat, 1 fruit

# Cinnamon Chicken Salad

The addition of cinnamon and cloves gives this chicken salad a unique taste.

**Dressing:**
**2 Tbl. reduced calorie mayonnaise**
**2 Tbl. nonfat yogurt (plain)**
**1/2 tsp. cinnamon**
**1/8 tsp. ground cloves**
**1/8 tsp. black pepper**
**1/8 tsp. salt (optional)**

**2 cups cooked and cubed chicken or turkey**
**1/2 cup sliced celery**
**1 cup seedless grapes**
**8 large lettuce leaves**

Mix first six ingredients for dressing. Combine chicken, celery and grapes. Top with dressing and mix well. Serve on lettuce.

Yield: about 4 cups (4 servings)
One serving: 1 cup
Calories per serving: 175
Exchanges: 3 lean meat, 1/2 fruit

# Rice, Potatoes, & Pasta

See the section on *Meatless Dishes* for more pasta dishes. Also see the section on *Stuffed Potatoes*.

# Herb Rice Blend

Quick cooking brown rice makes this a quick dish. The addition of herbs adds a great flavor without additional calories. See Nutrient Analysis to compare sodium using regular and salt free bouillon. Herb and Vegetable Rice Blend is a variation of this recipe.

**2 tsp. instant beef or chicken bouillon**
**2 cups water**
**1/8 tsp. dried rosemary**
**1/4 tsp. dried marjoram**
**1/4 tsp. dried thyme**
**1 tsp. dried onion**
**1 cup quick cooking brown rice**

Mix first six ingredients in a saucepan. Bring to a boil. Add rice and reduce heat to low. Cover and simmer for 12-14 minutes.

Yield: about 2 cups (4 servings)
One serving: 1/2 cup
Calories per serving: 110
Exchanges: 1 1/2 starch

Variation: Substitute 3/4 tsp. Italian herb seasoning for rosemary, marjoram and thyme.

# Herb and Vegetable Rice Blend

You can vary the vegetables if you want more color or crunch. This is a good way to change a plain rice dish.

**1 recipe Herb Rice Blend (page 112)**
**1 cup cooked, sliced vegetables (such as mushrooms, celery, etc.)**

Prepare one full recipe of Herb Rice Blend. Add hot vegetables and mix well.

Yield: about 3 cups (4 servings)
One serving: 3/4 cup
Calories per serving: 120
Exchanges: 1 1/2 starch

# Low Fat French Fries

This is a children's favorite that is so easy to prepare!

**4  medium potatoes (5 oz. each)**
**1 Tbl. oil (canola or olive)**
**salt to taste (optional)**
**malt vinegar to taste**

Preheat oven to 475 degrees. Scrub potatoes but don't peel. Cut into half inch slices or strips. Place potato slices in a plastic bag with the oil and shake well to coat potatoes evenly. Spray baking sheet with a non-stick cooking spray. Arrange potatoes in a single layer and bake for 30 minutes, or until golden brown, turning potatoes every 10 minutes. Sprinkle with salt (optional), and serve with malt vinegar.

Yield: 4 servings
One serving: 1/4 recipe
Calories per serving: 185
Exchanges: 2 starch, 1/2 fat

Variation: Temperature may be decreased to 450 degrees and baking time increased to 40 minutes.

# Microwave Baked Potatoes

This method reduces the conventional oven cooking time by two thirds.  You'll find several recipes in this book using baked potatoes and adding a topping.  All work well for a main dish.

**4  medium potatoes ( 5 oz. each)**

Scrub potatoes.  Prick each potato three times with a fork.  Arrange in a circle on a paper towel in the microwave, at least one inch apart.  Cook on high for 10-13 minutes, turning over and rotating 1/4 turn halfway through cooking time. Wrap in a towel and let stand 5-10 minutes to complete cooking.

Yield: 4  medium potatoes (4 servings)
One serving: 1 medium potato
Calories per serving: 150
Exchanges: 2 starch

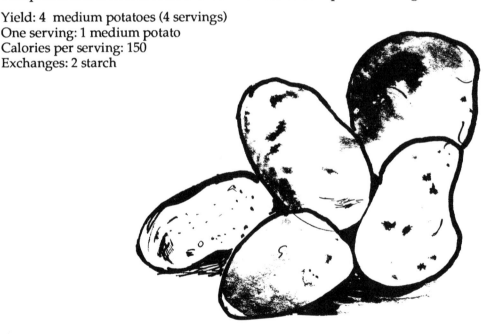

# Scalloped Potatoes

This is easy to assemble and quick cooking if you're using a microwave. However, if you're not in a hurry and you have something else in the oven, you'll find it is just as easy to use the oven. See the variations below to make this a main dish.

**4 medium potatoes (about 4 cups, sliced)**
**2 Tbl. flour**
**1 Tbl. dried onion**
**1 tsp. Molly McButter**
**1/4 tsp. pepper**
**1 1/2 cups skim milk**

Scrub potatoes. Without peeling, cut into 1/4 inch slices. Layer in a 2 1/2-quart casserole dish that has been sprayed with non-stick coating. Sprinkle each layer with Molly McButter, pepper, onion and flour. Pour milk over top. Cook in microwave or conventional oven.

**Microwave Method:** Cook, covered, 15-18 minutes, stirring every 4 minutes. Be sure to use a container twice the size of the contents to prevent a boil over.

**Conventional Oven:** Preheat oven to 350 degrees. Bake uncovered about 1 1/4 hours. Stir two to three times during cooking.

Yield: 6 servings
One serving: 1/6 recipe
Calories per serving: 115
Exchanges: 1 1/2 starch

Variations: To make this into a main dish, add cubed ham or smoked turkey sausage before the end of cooking time and heat thoroughly.
Top with 2 oz. grated, low fat cheese or sprinkle with cheese flavored Molly McButter.

# Tomato and Basil Pasta

Fresh tomatoes and basil add a wonderful flavor to this light dish.

**2 large tomatoes, diced (2 cups)**
**1 tsp. dried basil**
**1 tsp. chopped garlic**
**1/2 tsp. salt (optional)**
**1/8 tsp. pepper**
**6 oz. angel hair pasta**
**Parmesan cheese (optional)**

Mix first five ingredients and let sit at room temperature at least one hour. Cook angel hair pasta according to package directions, omitting oil and salt. Drain pasta and add tomato mixture. Serve immediately and top with Parmesan cheese (optional).

Yield: about 4 cups (4 servings)
One serving: 1 cups
Calories per serving: 170
Exchanges: 2 starch, 1 vegetable

# Sandwiches, Pizza, & Stuffed Potatoes

# Fruit and Ricotta Sandwich

Serve this for a quick breakfast or lunch. Sliced peaches or pears are good on this sandwich.

**1 slice whole wheat toast**
**1/4 cup low fat Ricotta cheese**
**1/2 cup sliced fruit (canned or fresh)**
**1/8 tsp. cinnamon**

Spread cheese on toast. Top with fruit. Sprinkle with cinnamon. Broil until fruit is hot.

Yield: 1 sandwich
One serving: 1 sandwich
Calories per serving: 155
Exchanges: 1 starch, 1 lean meat, 1/2 fruit

# Tomato and Ricotta Sandwich

This is another quick sandwich for lunch. The addition of mustard adds a good flavor.

**1 slice whole wheat toast**
**1/4 cup low fat Ricotta cheese**
**2 tomato slices**
**1/2 tsp. Dijon mustard**

Spread cheese on toast. Top with tomato. Spread mustard on tomato. Broil until tomato is hot.

Yield: 1 sandwich
One serving: 1 sandwich
Calories per serving: 130
Exchanges: 1 starch, 1 lean meat

# Turkey French Dips

Leftover turkey or sliced turkey from the deli is good in this sandwich. If you're in a hurry you can heat the sandwiches in the microwave but they won't be as crusty as this oven version.

**4 oz. cooked turkey slices**
**4 (6 inch) French rolls**
**4 oz. part skim mozzarella cheese**
**1 package French's Au Jus Gravy Mix**

Preheat oven to 400 degrees. Cut French rolls lengthwise. Place 1 oz. turkey and 1 oz. mozzarella cheese on each French roll. Wrap each roll in aluminum foil and heat in the oven for 10 minutes. Mix au jus according to package directions, or add more water to reduce the sodium content. Slice each sandwich in half, diagonally. Serve each with 1/3 cup au jus.

Yield: 4 sandwiches (4 servings)
One serving: 1 sandwich and 1/3 cup au jus
Calories per serving: 355
Exchanges: 2 lean meat, 3 starch

Variation: Omit cheese and use 2 oz. turkey.

# Meatball Sandwich

This is another recipe using the Baked Meatballs in this book.

**4  four-inch French rolls**
**12 meatballs (page 196)**
**1 cup Ragu Homestyle Spaghetti Sauce**

Heat meatballs in sauce.  Slit rolls open being careful not to cut through the last half inch.  Fill each roll with 3 meatballs and 1/4 of the sauce.

Yield: 4 sandwiches
One serving: 1 sandwich
Calories per serving: turkey-303; beef-317
Exchanges: 2 1/4 starch, 1 1/2 medium fat meat, 1 vegetable


# Boboli Pizza - Sausage Style

The turkey sausage is a good substitute for pepperoni.  Be sure to slice it paper thin.  Add pineapple or sliced vegetables for more variety.

**1 (16 oz.) Boboli Italian Bread Shell**
**1/2 cup Ragu 100% Natural Pizza Sauce**
**1 tsp. Italian herb seasoning**
**4 oz. Turkey Smoked Sausage (such as Louis Rich)**
**4 oz. grated, low fat cheese (mozzarella or cheddar)**

Preheat oven to 450 degrees.  Place Boboli on pizza pan.  Spoon on pizza sauce, sprinkle with Italian herbs and cheese.  Slice sausage extra thin and arrange over cheese.  Bake for 8-10 minutes or until cheese is melted.

Yield: 16 slices (8 servings)
Serving size: 2 slices
Calories per serving: 220
Exchanges: 2 starch, 1 medium fat meat

# Boboli Pizza - Shrimp Style

Seafood cocktail sauce adds a different taste to a traditional food.  This would also be good as an hors d'oeuvre.

**1 (16 oz.) Boboli Italian Bread Shell**
**1/2 cup seafood cocktail sauce**
**4 oz. low fat cheese (mozzarella or cheddar)**
**2 cups cooked shrimp (frozen works well)**

Preheat oven to 450 degrees.  Place Boboli on pizza pan.  Spoon on the cocktail sauce, and add cheese.  Arrange shrimp over cheese.  Bake for 8-10 minutes or until cheese is melted.

Yield: 16 slices (8 servings)
Serving size: 2 slices
Calories per serving: 240
Exchanges: 2 starch, 1 1/2 lean meat

Variation: Add thinly sliced green pepper, onions, mushrooms or tomatoes.

# Crusty Calzone

This is especially quick to put together if you remember to thaw the bread dough overnight! Four different fillings are listed and you can probably think of more.

**Crust:**
**1 lb. frozen bread dough, thawed and at room temperature***
**1/4 cup Ragu 100% Natural Pizza Sauce**
**1/2 tsp. garlic powder**
**1/4 tsp. Italian herb seasoning**

**Turkey Sausage Filling:**
**1/2 lb. turkey smoked sausage, sliced very thin**
**1/2 onion, sliced**
**1 green pepper, sliced**
**4 oz. grated, low fat cheese (mozzarella or cheddar)**

Preheat oven to 425 degrees. Roll dough into 10-inch by 14-inch rectangle and place on baking sheet that has been sprayed with non-stick coating. Spread pizza sauce on half of the dough, and sprinkle with garlic powder and Italian Seasoning. Top with filling ingredients. Fold dough over and press edges together to seal in filling. Bake for 20 minutes.

Yield: 8 slices (8 servings)
One serving: 1 slice
Calories per serving: 230
Exchanges: 2 starch, 1 medium fat meat

* Thaw frozen bread dough in refrigerator overnight, then set out for about 1/2 hour at room temperature for easier rolling.

## ALTERNATE FILLINGS FOR CRUSTY CALZONE

**Ground Meat Filling:**
   1/2 lb. extra lean ground beef (9% fat or less) or ground turkey(7% fat) ,
   cooked and crumbled
   1 cup sliced vegetables
   4 oz. grated, low fat cheese

Yield: 8 slices (8 servings)
One serving: 1 slice
Calories per serving: turkey-235; beef-245
Exchanges: 2 starch, 1 medium fat meat

**Turkey Ham Filling:**
   1/2 lb. sliced turkey ham
   1/2 cup drained pineapple chunks (unsweetened)
   4 oz. grated, low fat cheese

Yield: 8 slices (8 servings)
One serving: 1 slice
Calories per serving: 225
Exchanges: 2 starch, 1 medium fat meat

**Sliced Turkey Filling:**
   1/2 lb. sliced turkey
   1/2 cup sliced mushrooms
   4 oz. grated, low fat cheese

Yield: 8 slices (8 servings)
One serving: 1 slice
Calories per serving: 230
Exchanges: 2 starch, 1 medium fat meat

# Focaccia Pizza

I keep several loaves of Focaccia bread in my freezer so I can make this recipe in a moment's notice. Add your favorite pizza toppings, avoiding the high-fat pepperoni and emphasizing lean meats and vegetables.

**1 loaf (1 lb.) Focaccia bread**
**1/2 cup Ragu 100% Natural Pizza Sauce**
**4 oz. part skim mozzarella cheese**

Preheat oven to 375 degrees. Cut the bread in half, horizontally, so that you have two round loaves. Place on baking sheet. Top each with pizza sauce and cheese. Add your favorite toppings. Bake for 20 minutes.

Yield: 8 slices (8 servings)
One serving: 1 slice
Calories per serving: 205
Exchanges: 2 starch, 1/2 medium fat meat

# Individual Pizza

This is another quick pizza recipe. Try this one for a quick after school snack.

**3/4 cup Ragu 100% Natural Pizza Sauce**
**1 oz. grated, part skim mozzarella cheese**
**1 oz. grated, low fat cheddar cheese**
**2 (6 inch) French rolls**
**1/4 cup thinly sliced green pepper**
**1/4 cup thinly sliced onion**

Preheat oven to 475 degrees. Cut French rolls in half and spread pizza sauce over each half. Top with cheeses and vegetables. Bake for 15 minutes or until cheese is melted.

Yield: 4 pizzas (4 servings)
One serving: 1 pizza
Calories per serving: 180
Exchanges: 1 1/2 starch, 1 vegetable, 1/2 medium fat meat

# Cheese and Chicken - Potato Topping

This is a good recipe for using leftover chicken or turkey.

**4 medium potatoes (5 oz. each)**
**1 cup chopped broccoli flowerets**
**1 cup cooked and cubed chicken or turkey**
**1 tsp. instant chicken bouillon**
**1/2 tsp. dried onion**
**1/4 tsp. dry mustard**
**1/8 tsp. paprika**
**1 1/2 Tbl. flour**
**3/4 cup skim milk**
**1 oz.  grated, low fat cheddar cheese**

Scrub potatoes.  Bake in oven or cook in microwave.  Prepare topping using a method below. Cut potatoes in half and flake center with fork. Spoon 1/4 of the topping over two potato halves. Top with cheese and return to microwave (30-60 seconds) or  hot oven (5 minutes) until cheese is melted.

**Microwave Method:** In a 2-qt. casserole, microwave broccoli on high for 1-2 minutes, or until tender crisp. Add turkey, and heat for 45 seconds on high.  In a medium bowl, mix bouillon, onion, mustard, paprika, and flour.  Add milk slowly, using a wire whip to prevent lumps. Microwave on high 3-4 minutes, stirring several times until thickened. Add milk mixture to turkey and broccoli. Fill potatoes as described above.

**Stovetop Method:** In a covered container, shake flour with milk to prevent lumps. Add bouillon, onion, mustard and paprika. Cook over low heat, stirring constantly, until thickened. Set aside. Stir-fry broccoli, in a skillet that has been sprayed with non-stick coating, to desired tenderness.  Add turkey and milk mixture. Heat thoroughly.  Fill potatoes as described above.

Yield: 4  servings
One serving: 1 medium potato and 1/4 topping
Calories per serving: 260
Exchanges: 2  starch, 1 1/2 lean meat, 1 vegetable

# Cheese Stuffed Potatoes

This is a potato dish that kids like.  Serve two halves if this is the main part of the meal.

**4 medium baked potatoes, 5 oz. each (still warm)**
**1 cup low fat cottage cheese or low fat Ricotta cheese**
**4 tsp. skim milk**
**2 Tbl. chopped green onion**
**1/4 tsp. paprika**

Slice each potato in half, lengthwise.  Scoop out pulp, leaving about 1/4 inch thick shells.  Blend cheese, milk, onion.  Add potato and mix until smooth.  Fill potato shell halves with mixture.  Arrange on a baking dish and sprinkle with paprika.

**Microwave Method:** Cover with wax paper.  Heat on high for 5 minutes, turning 1/4 turn halfway through cooking.

**Conventional Oven:** Preheat oven to 350 degrees.  Bake for 10-15 minutes or until thoroughly heated.

Yield: 8 servings
One serving: 1 potato half
Calories per serving: 100
Exchanges: 1 starch, 1/2 lean meat

# Ground Meat and Mushroom - Potato Topping

This is especially quick if you use the microwave to bake the potatoes. The topping is easy to put together and fast to cook using either the microwave or stovetop method. Canned mushrooms can be substituted for fresh.

**4 medium potatoes (5 oz. each)**
**1/2 lb. ground beef (9% fat or less) or ground turkey (7% fat)**
**1 small onion, chopped**
**8 oz. fresh mushrooms, sliced**
**1/4 tsp. chopped garlic**
**1/3 cup skim milk**
**1/3 cup tomato juice***
**1 Tbl. cornstarch**
**1/4 tsp. salt (optional)**
**1/4 tsp. dry mustard**
**1/8 tsp. pepper**

Scrub potatoes, and bake in microwave, or conventional oven. Prepare topping using the microwave or stovetop method listed below. Cut potatoes in half and flake center with a fork. Spoon 1/4 of the mixture over two potato halves.

**Microwave Method:** In a 2-qt. casserole, combine crumbled ground meat, onion, mushrooms and garlic. Cover and microwave on high for 3-6 minutes, or until meat is done, stirring several times during cooking. Combine remaining ingredients and stir into meat mixture. Microwave on high for 4-7 minutes until mixture thickens, stirring several times. Fill potatoes as described above.

**Stovetop Method:** Brown meat, with next three ingredients, in a skillet that has been sprayed with non-stick coating. Combine remaining ingredients and stir into meat mixture. Cook stirring constantly, until mixture thickens. Fill potatoes as described above.

Yield: 4 servings
One serving: 1 medium potato and 1/4 topping
Calories per serving: turkey-290; beef-305
Exchanges: 1 1/2 medium fat meat, 2 starch, 1 vegetable

*Sodium is figured for salt-free.

# Pizza - Potato Topping

This is a dish your children will enjoy.  Serve this quick meal with a salad or sliced fruit.

4 medium potatoes (5 oz. each)
1/2 lb. ground beef (9% fat or less) or ground turkey (7% fat)
1 small onion, chopped
1/2 cup chopped green pepper
1 large tomato, chopped
2 Tbl. catsup
1/2 tsp. salt (optional)
1/8 tsp. pepper
1/2 tsp. Italian herb seasoning
1 oz. grated, low fat cheese (mozzarella or cheddar)

Scrub potatoes and bake in oven or microwave.  Prepare topping using the microwave or stovetop method listed below.  Cut potatoes in half and flake center with a fork.  Spoon 1/4 of the mixture over two potato halves.  Top with grated cheese.  Return to microwave (30-60 seconds) or hot oven (5 minutes) until cheese is melted.

**Microwave Method:**  In a 2-qt. casserole, combine crumbled ground meat, onion, and green pepper.  Microwave on high for 3- 4 minutes or until meat is done, stirring several times during cooking.  Stir in remaining ingredients, except cheese.  Heat on high for 1 minute.  Fill potatoes as described above.

**Stovetop Method:**  Brown meat with next two ingredients in a skillet that has been sprayed with non-stick coating.  Add remaining ingredients, except cheese, and heat thoroughly.  Fill potatoes as described above.

Yield: 4 servings
One serving: 1 medium potato and 1/4  topping
Calories per serving: turkey-300; beef-310
Exchanges: 1 1/2 medium fat meat, 2 starch, 1 vegetable

# Meatless Entrees

# Fruit and Ricotta Split

Try this for a snack or as part of a light lunch. The fruit and cheese combination is really good.

**1/2 small banana**
**1/2 cup strawberries**
**1/2 cup low fat Ricotta cheese**
**sweetener to taste**

Cut banana lengthwise and open onto a plate. Top with cheese. Sweeten strawberries to taste and spoon over cheese.

Yield: 1 serving
One serving: 1 recipe
Calories per serving: 185
Exchanges: 2 lean meat, 1 1/4 fruit

# Egg Foo Yung

This recipe is very quick. Be sure to serve it with the sauce as it really adds flavor. See Nutrient Analysis to compare sodium using regular or salt free broth.

**1 cup egg substitute (equal to 4 eggs)**
**1 can (16 oz.) Chinese vegetables (unsalted), drained**

Prepare Foo Yung Sauce (below) and keep warm. Pour eggs into a heated 10-inch teflon pan that has been sprayed with non-stick coating. Spread vegetables over eggs and continue cooking until eggs begin to set. Broil just until top is golden. Serve with sauce.

## Foo Yung Sauce:
**1 Tbl. cornstarch**
**1 cup beef broth, fat free**
**1/2 tsp. soy sauce**

**Stovetop Method:** Mix ingredients and stir over medium heat until mixture thickens and boils.

**Microwave Method:** Mix ingredients and heat on high for 2-3 minutes, stirring halfway, until mixture boils.

Yield: 4 servings
One serving: 1/4 the recipe
Calories per serving: 60
Exchanges*: 1 lean meat, 1 vegetable

*Due to the low fat content of Egg Beaters egg substitute, the calories are less than the exchanges would compute.

# Spanish Zucchini Frittata

This is one of my favorites omelets because I like chiles and salsa combined with eggs.

**4 cups unpeeled, grated zucchini (about 1 1/2 lbs.)**
**2 Tbl. chopped onion**
**1/2 tsp. chopped garlic**
**1 can (4 oz.) diced green chiles**
**1 cup egg substitute (equal to 4 eggs)**
**2 Tbl. skim milk**
**1/2 tsp. cumin**
**1/2 tsp. chili powder**
**1/4 tsp. pepper**
**1/2 tsp. salt (optional)**
**salsa (optional)**

Spray a 10-inch skillet with non-stick coating. Sauté first three ingredients until zucchini is tender, pouring off any liquid. Add chiles. Meanwhile, mix eggs, milk, and seasonings. Add to the zucchini mixture and cook until the eggs begin to set. Broil just until top is golden. Serve with salsa.

Yield: 4 servings
One serving: 1/4 omelet
Calories per serving: 60
Exchanges*: 1 lean meat, 1 vegetable

*Due to the low fat content of Egg Beaters egg substitute, the calories are less than the exchanges would compute.

# Italian Zucchini Frittata

This is a good way to use zucchini in an omelet and it is a delicious supper.

**4 cups unpeeled, grated zucchini (about 1 1/2 lbs.)**
**2 Tbl. chopped onion**
**1/2 tsp. chopped garlic**
**1 cup egg substitute (equal to 4 eggs)**
**2 Tbl. skim milk**
**1/2 tsp. dried oregano**
**1/2 tsp. dried basil**
**1/4 tsp. pepper**
**1/2 tsp. salt (optional)**
**2 Tbl. Parmesan cheese**

Spray a 10-inch skillet with a non-stick coating. Sauté first three ingredients until zucchini is tender, pouring off any liquid. Meanwhile, mix eggs, milk and seasonings (except cheese). Add to the zucchini mixture and cook until the eggs begin to set. Top with Parmesan cheese. Broil just until top is golden.

Yield: 4 servings
One serving: 1/4 omelet
Calories per serving: 65
Exchanges*: 1 lean meat, 1 vegetable

*Due to the low fat content of Egg Beaters egg substitute, the calories are less than the exchanges would compute.

# Puffy Chile Relleno Casserole

I like this recipe for brunch but it is also good for dinner.  Serve it with sliced oranges and grapefruit sections.

**3 cans (7 oz. each) whole green chiles**
**8 flour tortillas (6-inch size), cut into 1" strips**
**1 lb. grated low fat cheese (mozzarella or cheddar)**
**3 cups egg substitute (equal to 12 eggs)**
**3/4 cup skim milk**
**1/2 tsp. each: pepper, cumin, garlic powder**
**1/4 tsp. salt (optional)**
**1 tsp. paprika**
**salsa (optional)**

Preheat oven to 350 degrees.  Drain chiles and remove seeds.  Spray a 9-inch by 13-inch pan with non-stick coating.  Lay half the chiles in the pan.  Top with half the tortilla strips and then half the cheese.  Repeat another layer using remaining chiles, tortillas, and cheese.  Beat remaining ingredients (except paprika) and pour over casserole. Sprinkle with paprika. Bake uncovered for 40 minutes or until puffy and set in the center.  Let stand 10 minutes before serving.  Serve with salsa.

Yield: 8 servings
One serving: 1/8 of recipe
Calories per serving: 295
Exchanges: 1 starch, 1 vegetable, 3 lean meat, 1/2 fat

# Italian Broccoli and Pasta

This has a great flavor. Try adding shrimp for variety.

**2 cups broccoli flowerets**
**3 Tbl. chopped green onion**
**1/2 tsp. dried thyme**
**1/2 tsp. dried oregano**
**1/2 tsp. pepper**
**1 can (14 1/2 oz.) stewed tomatoes,\* not drained**
**2 cups uncooked fettucini noodles (eggless)**
**2 tsp. Parmesan cheese**

Cook fettucini according to package instructions (omitting oil and salt) and drain. Spray a skillet with non-stick spray and stir-fry onion and broccoli for 3 minutes. Add seasonings and tomatoes and simmer until heated throughout. Spoon vegetable mixture over fettucini and top with Parmesan cheese.

Yield: 3 cups vegetable sauce, 2 cups fettucine (4 servings)
One serving: 3/4 cup sauce, 1/2 cup fettucini, 1/2 tsp. Parmesan cheese
Calories per serving: 150
Exchanges: 1 starch, 2 1/2 vegetables

\* Sodium is figured for canned without salt.

# Vegetables Primavera

Children may not like all the vegetables in this recipe, but adults sure do.  Top with Parmesan cheese when serving.

**4 cups vegetables, any combination of the following:**
   **chopped:  broccoli, cauliflower, celery, cabbage, onions, or green peppers**
   **sliced:  mushrooms, or carrots**
   **pea pods**
   **green beans**
**1 jar (28 oz.) Ragu Homestyle Spaghetti Sauce (without meat)**
**2 1/2 cups cooked spaghetti noodles**

**Microwave method:** Mix all ingredients, cover and cook on high for 15 minutes, stirring at 5 minute intervals.  Cook longer if you prefer vegetables to be less crisp.  Serve over spaghetti noodles.

**Stovetop method:** Mix all ingredients, cover and simmer until vegetables are cooked to preferred tenderness.  Serve over spaghetti noodles.

Yield: about 4 cups vegetable sauce and 2 1/2 cups noodles (5 servings)
One serving: 3/4 cup of vegetable sauce and 1/2 cup of noodles
Calories per serving: 220
Exchanges: 2 vegetable, 2 starch

# Quick Lasagne

You don't precook the noodles in this recipe so it is really fast to assemble. This can be put together the night before and refrigerated without baking. Increase baking time by 15 minutes if it has been refrigerated.

4 cups Ragu Homestyle Spaghetti Sauce (without meat)
2 cups low fat Ricotta cheese
1 cup low fat cottage cheese
2 Tbl. dried parsley
1 tsp. chopped garlic
4 oz. grated, part skim mozzarella cheese
3/4 lb. uncooked lasagne noodles
1/4 cup Parmesan cheese

Preheat oven to 350 degrees. Spray a 9-inch by 13-inch pan with non-stick coating. Mix Ricotta cheese, cottage cheese, parsley, and garlic. Pour 1 cup of sauce in bottom of pan. Arrange 1/3 of the noodles in the pan so that they touch but do not overlap. Spread 1/2 of the cheese mixture over the noodles. Top with 1/2 of the mozzarella cheese. Top this with 1 cup of sauce, 1/3 of the noodles, the remainder of the cheese mixture and the rest of the mozzarella cheese. Add another cup of sauce, another layer of noodles, and the remainder of the sauce. Sprinkle with Parmesan cheese. Bake, covered tightly with aluminum foil, for one hour.

Yield: 12 servings
One serving: 1/12 recipe
Calories per serving: 240
Exchanges: 1 1/2 starch, 2 vegetable, 1 lean meat

# *P*oultry

Poultry is a lean choice if the skin and extra fat is removed. Keep some boneless, skinless pieces in the freezer for quick meals.

Frozen, precooked, diced chicken is available in many areas. This is a good choice for casseroles. However, you can cook a turkey breast, have slices for a meal, and dice the remainder for casseroles. Also, the recipe in this section entitled *Cooked and Cubed Chicken* is an easy one for preparing chicken for casseroles.

The *Nutrient Analysis of Recipes* in this book uses data for breasts which is lower in fat than other chicken parts. Most of the recipes have a notation stating that the calories are less than the *Exchanges* would compute. This is because chicken breasts have about one gram of fat per ounce instead if the three grams of fat used in the *Exchange List* for the lean meat group.

# Cooked and Cubed Chicken

Many recipes call for cooked chicken. You can use leftover turkey or leftover chicken. But when leftovers are not available, it is easy to microwave or simmer chicken. Follow one of the directions below and consider cooking extra and freezing for future use.

**1 3/4 lbs. boneless, skinless chicken breasts**

**Microwave Method:** Cut breasts into 1-inch strips. Arrange on a baking dish in a circle on the outer portion of the dish. Cover with wax paper and microwave on high for 5 minutes, rearranging halfway through cooking time. Let sit a few minutes before cutting into bite size pieces.

**Stovetop Method:** Place chicken in a pan and cover with water. Cover and simmer on low until tender (about 15-20 minutes). Drain liquid. Cut into bite size pieces.

Yield: about 4 cups, cooked and cubed (8 servings)
One serving: 1/2 cup
Calories per serving: 110
Exchanges*: 3 lean meat

*Due to the low fat content of chicken breasts, the calories are less than the exchanges would compute.

Cooked and cubed chicken is used in the following recipes:
Cheese and Chicken-Potato Topping
Cinnamon Chicken
Chicken Enchiladas
Chicken Fruit Salad
Chicken Spinach Salad
Mexican Chicken Casserole
Baked Chimichangas

# Baked Chimichangas

This is a favorite for those of us who like Mexican food. Sodium is figured for bottled salsa. To reduce the sodium, use the salsa recipe in this book.

**8 six-inch flour tortillas**

**Filling:**
**1 1/2 cups cooked and cubed chicken**
**2 oz. grated, low fat cheese**
**3/4 cup salsa, thick and chunky**
**Optional:  extra salsa**
            **Spanish Yogurt Dressing (recipe in this book)**

Preheat oven to 400 degrees. Mix filling ingredients. Warm tortillas until pliable (about 5 seconds each in microwave or in a non-stick skillet).  Wet one side of tortilla and place wet side down. Spoon on filling ingredients.  Fold to hold in filling. Spray baking dish with non-stick coating.  Lay chimichangas, seam side down, on baking dish.  Bake for 15 minutes.

Yield: 8 chimichangas ( 4 servings)
One serving: 2 chimichangas
Calories per serving: 275
Exchanges: 2 starch, 2 lean meat

Variations: Divide filling onto four large tortillas. Substitute ground or diced beef, pork, or turkey for chicken.

# Chicken Enchiladas

This recipe can be layered to save time or you can fill each tortilla and roll in the traditional way.  Turkey, pork, or beef can be substituted for the chicken.  Top each serving with Spanish Yogurt Dressing.

**2 cups cooked and cubed chicken**
**1 cup chopped onion**
**1 cup low fat Ricotta cheese**
**1 cup nonfat plain yogurt**
**2 oz. grated, low fat cheddar cheese**
**2 oz. grated, part skim mozzarella cheese**
**12 corn tortillas**
**2 cans (10 oz. each) enchilada sauce**

Preheat oven to 375 degrees.  Mix first six ingredients and set aside.

Spray a 9-inch by 13-inch baking dish with non-stick cooking spray. Pour 1/2 can of enchilada sauce in bottom of pan.   Follow either method below for layered or rolled.  Bake for 20-30 minutes or until heated thoughly.

**Rolled Method:** Place about 1/3-1/2 cup filling on each tortilla and roll to enclose (cracks in tortillas are not as noticeable after cooking).  Place seam side down in baking dish. Top with remaining sauce.

**Layered Method:** Follow this order: 1/3 of the tortillas, 1/2 of the filling, 1/3 tortillas, 1  can of sauce, remainder of filling, remainder of tortillas, remainder of sauce.

Yield: 8 servings
One serving: 1/8 recipe
Calories per serving: 275
Exchanges: 1 1/2 starch, 2 1/2 lean meat, 1 vegetable

# Chicken Fajitas

This is a good family recipe.

**1 lb. boneless, skinless chicken breasts, cut into 1-inch strips**
**3 Tbl. lime juice**
**1/2 tsp. coriander**
**1/2 tsp. chili powder**
**1 green pepper, sliced**
**1 onion, sliced**
**8 flour tortillas (6 inch size)**
**salsa (optional)**

Mix lime juice with coriander and chili powder and pour over chicken. Set aside. Meanwhile, slice vegetables. Add to chicken and mix well. Spray pan with non-stick coating and stir-fry chicken and vegetables until done. Warm tortillas in microwave about 50 seconds on high or in non-stick skillet. Fill each tortilla with chicken mixture and serve with salsa.

Yield: 8 filled tortillas (4 servings)
One serving: 2 filled tortillas
Calories per serving: 320
Exchanges*: 4 lean meat, 2 starch, 1 vegetable

*Due to the low fat content of chicken breasts, the calories are less than the exchanges would compute.

# Chicken in Salsa

This is a favorite for salsa lovers.  Bottled salsa or the salsa recipe in this book can be used.  Sodium is figured using bottled salsa.  To reduce the sodium, use the salsa recipe in this book.

**1 lb. skinless, boneless chicken breasts**
**3/4 cup salsa**

Arrange chicken in a 9-inch by 9-inch pan that has been sprayed with non-stick coating.  Follow directions below for microwave or conventional oven.

**Conventional Oven:** Preheat oven to 350 degrees.  Bake, uncovered, for 20 minutes.  Spoon salsa over chicken.  Return to oven for 10 minutes or until chicken is done and salsa is heated.

**Microwave Method:** Cover with plastic wrap, venting one corner.  Cook on high for 6-8 minutes, depending on thickness of chicken.  Rotate 1/4 turn halfway through cooking time.  Drain any liquid.  Spoon salsa over chicken. Cook for 1-2 minutes or until salsa is heated.

Yield: 4 servings
One serving: 1/4 recipe
Calories per serving: 170
Exchanges*: 3 lean meat, 1 vegetable

*Due to the low fat content of chicken breasts, the calories are less than the exchanges would compute.

# Chicken Picadillo

Serve this in a tortilla or with French bread.  It is also good served with rice. Sodium is figured using bottled salsa. To reduce the sodium, use the salsa recipe in this book.

**1 lb. boneless, skinless chicken breasts**
**1 tsp. cumin**
**3/4 cup salsa, thick and chunky**
**1/2 tsp. chopped garlic**
**1 onion, sliced**
**1 green pepper, sliced**

Cut chicken into 1-inch strips. Sprinkle with cumin. Spray skillet with non-stick coating and stir-fry chicken until tender and no longer pink.  Add salsa, garlic, onion, and green pepper.  Cover and simmer for 10 minutes or until vegetables are tender.

Yield: 4 servings
One serving: 1/4 recipe
Calories per serving: 190
Exchanges*: 4 lean meat, 1 vegetable

*Due to the low fat content of chicken breasts, the calories are less than the exchanges would compute.

# Mexican Chicken Casserole

This is a popular dish to take to potlucks. It is also a good way to use up leftover turkey. Serve it with salsa or the Spanish Yogurt Dressing recipe in this book.

**2/3 cup Cream Soup Mix (page 70)**
**2 1/2 cups water**
**1/2 cup skim milk**
**1 tsp. cumin**
**1/2 tsp. chili powder**
**12 flour tortillas, cut into 1" strips**
**4  cups cooked and cubed chicken**
**1 cup diced onion or 4 Tbl. dried onion**
**2 cans (4 oz. each) diced green chiles**
**4 oz. grated low fat cheddar cheese**

Preheat oven to 350 degrees. In a 4-cup glass measuring cup, combine soup mix and water. Heat on high in microwave for 6-7 minutes, stirring every 2 minutes until bubbly (see page 70 for stovetop method). Add next three ingredients and set aside. Spray a 9-inch by 13-inch pan with non-stick cooking spray. Lay one third of the tortilla strips in the pan. Top with 1/2 the chicken, chiles, onion and 1/3 of the soup mixture. Repeat layering, ending with the tortillas and topping with the remaining soup mixture. Bake uncovered for 35-40 minutes. Top with cheese and bake for another 5 minutes.

Yield: 8 servings
One serving: 1/8 recipe
Calories per serving: 320
Exchanges: 3 lean meat, 1 1/2 starch, 1 vegetable

# Mexican Style Chicken and Rice

This recipe is a good combination of vegetables, chicken, and rice. Serve with a dollop of nonfat yogurt.

**1 medium onion, chopped**
**1 green pepper, chopped**
**1 tsp. minced garlic**
**1 can (16 oz.) canned tomatoes***
**1 can (4 oz.) chopped chiles**
**1 can (14 1/2 oz.) Swanson's chicken broth (30% less salt), fat removed**
**1 3/4 cups quick cooking brown rice**
**6 drops Tabasco sauce**
**2 lbs. boneless, skinless chicken breasts**
**2 oz. grated, low fat cheddar cheese**

Preheat oven to 350 degrees. Cook onion and pepper in a skillet that has been sprayed with non-stick coating. Add next six ingredients. Mix well and bring to a boil. Remove from heat and spoon into a 12-inch by 9-inch baking pan that has been sprayed with non-stick coating. Arrange chicken on top of rice mixture. Bake, covered, for 35 minutes or until rice is done. Sprinkle cheese over chicken. Let stand, 5 minutes or until cheese is melted.

Yield: 8 servings
One serving: 1/8 recipe
Calories per serving: 285
Exchanges**: 4 lean meat, 1 vegetable, 1 starch

*Sodium is figured for canned without salt.

**Due to the low fat content of chicken breasts, the calories are less than the exchanges would compute.

# Baked Chicken with Bottled Toppings

There are many bottled toppings that can be added to chicken during the last few minutes of cooking. They add variety and convenience. Keep several of these on hand. Some of these may be high in sodium, but you can significantly reduce the sodium by using less.

**1 lb. boneless, skinless chicken breasts**
**1/4 cup of one of the following bottled toppings:**
    **S & W Mesquite Cooking Sauce & Marinade**
    **Lea & Perrins White Wine Worcestershire Sauce**
    **Kraft Sauceworks Sweet'n Sour Sauce**
    **Ragu 100% Natural Pizza Sauce**
    **Old Spice Honey Mustard**
    **Milani 1890 Dill Sauce**

Arrange chicken in a 9-inch by 9-inch baking pan that has been sprayed with non-stick coating. Follow directions below for microwave or conventional oven.

**Oven Method:** Preheat oven to 350 degrees. Bake, uncovered, for 20 minutes. Top with 1/4 cup of one of the above toppings. Bake for 10 minutes or until chicken is done and sauce is heated.

**Microwave Method:** Cover with plastic wrap, venting one corner. Cook on high for 6-8 minutes, depending on thickness of chicken. Rotate 1/4 turn halfway through cooking time. Drain any liquid. Top chicken with 1/4 cup of one of the above toppings. Cook for 1-2 minutes or until sauce is heated.

Yield: 4 servings
One serving: 1/4 the recipe
Calories for 1/4 of the chicken (excluding topping): 150
Exchange*: 4 lean meat

*Due to the low fat content of chicken breasts, the calories are less than the exchanges would compute.

## CALORIES AND EXCHANGES FOR 1 TBL. OF THE FOLLOWING:

**Lea & Perrins White Wine Worcestershire Sauce**
Calories: 9        Exchanges: "free"

**Kraft Suaceworks Sweet'n Sour Sauce**
Calories: 25       Exchanges: 1/2 fruit

**Ragu 100% Natural Pizza Sauce**
Calories: 8        Exchanges: "free"

**Old Spice Honey Mustard**
Calories: 35       Exchanges: 1/2 fruit

**Milani 1890 Dill Sauce**
Calories: 1        Exchanges: "free"

Nutrient information was not available for **S & W Mesquite Cooking Sauce and Marinade.**

## Chicken á la Soda

Chicken prepared this way is very moist. The addition of vegetables adds to the flavor.

**1 1/2 lbs. boneless, skinless chicken breasts or 2 1/2 lbs. skinless chicken parts (with bone)**
**1 medium onion, sliced**
**1 green pepper, sliced**
**1 can (4 oz.) sliced mushrooms, drained**
**1/2 tsp. salt (optional)**
**1/8 tsp. pepper**
**1 can sugar-free orange soda pop**

Preheat oven to 350 degrees. Arrange chicken in a 3-quart casserole and top with remaining ingredients. Cover and bake for 35-45 minutes, or until chicken is tender. Uncover and bake 10 minutes.

Yield: 6 servings
One serving: 1/6 recipe
Calories per serving: 160
Exchanges*: 4 lean meat, 1 vegetable

*Due to the low fat content of chicken breasts, the calories are less than the exchanges would compute.

Variations: Add 2 cups sliced potatoes before cooking. Add other vegetables such as carrots, celery, etc.

# Chicken and Pea Pod Stir-Fry

This recipe has a light cornstarch gravy. It is especially good if you stir-fry the vegetables so that they are still crisp. Fresh broccoli or frozen pea pods can be substituted for the fresh pea pods.

**1 lb. boneless, skinless chicken breasts**
**1 1/2 Tbl. soy sauce**
**2 Tbl. dry sherry**
**1 Tbl. cornstarch**
**1/2 cup cold water**
**2 1/2 tsp. chopped garlic**
**3 carrots, sliced diagonally**
**2 packages frozen pea pods (6 oz. each), partially thawed**
**4 green onions, sliced**

Cut chicken into bite size pieces. Set aside. In a small bowl combine soy sauce, sherry, cornstarch, garlic, and water. Set aside. Spray a large skillet with a non-stick coating. Add carrots and stir-fry for 3 minutes. Add pea pods and onions. Stir-fry 2 minutes or until vegetables are crisp tender. Remove vegetables. Stir-fry chicken until no longer pink (use 2 Tbl. water if sticking to pan). Set aside. Pour cornstarch mixture into skillet and stir until thickened and bubbly. Add vegetables and chicken. Cover and cook 1 minute.

Yield: 5 servings
One serving: 1/5 recipe
Calories per serving: 190
Exchange*: 3 lean meat, 2 vegetable

*Due to the low fat content of chicken breasts, the calories are less than the exchanges compute.

# Chicken Breasts Florentine

I recommend serving this dish for company. It can be be assembled up to the point of baking and then refrigerated. Be sure to increase baking time by 15 minutes if it has been refrigerated.

**2 packages (10 oz. each) frozen chopped spinach**
**1 cup water**
**1 1/2 lbs. boneless, skinless chicken breasts**
**1/2 stalk celery**
**1/2 small onion**
**1/2 tsp. salt (optional)**
**3 Tbl. flour**
**1/2 cup milk**
**1/4 cup Parmesan cheese**
**1/8 tsp. nutmeg**

Preheat oven to 375 degrees. Cook spinach according to package directions. Drain well. Simmer chicken in water with the celery, onion, and salt until chicken is no longer pink (about 15 minutes). Remove chicken, reserving 1 cup of liquid and discarding vegetables. Shake flour with milk in a covered container to prevent lumps. Mix with reserved liquid in saucepan. Cook, stirring constantly, until thickened. Stir in nutmeg and cheese. Mix spinach with 1/2 of the sauce and spread in a 9-inch by 13-inch pan that has been sprayed with non-stick coating. Arrange chicken over spinach. Pour remainder of sauce over chicken. Sprinkle top with additional nutmeg, if desired. Bake, uncovered, for 25-30 minutes or until heated throughout.

Yield: 6 servings
One serving: 1/6 recipe
Calories per serving: 210
Exchanges*: 4 lean meat, 1 vegetable

*Due to the low fat content of chicken breasts, the calories are less than the exchanges compute.

# Chicken Breasts in Mushroom Sauce

The sherry and yogurt add a good flavor to this recipe.

**2 cups sliced mushrooms**
**1/4 cup chopped green onion**
**2 Tbl. flour**
**1/4 cup water**
**2 Tbl. dry sherry**
**1/2 cup plain nonfat yogurt**
**1/4 tsp. salt (optional)**
**1/8 tsp. pepper**
**1 tsp. instant chicken bouillon**
**1 lb. skinless, boneless chicken breasts**
**1/4 tsp. paprika**

**Microwave:** Combine mushrooms and onions in a 1 qt. casserole. Cover and cook on high for 3-4 minutes (stirring halfway) or until mushrooms are tender. Drain. Shake flour with water to prevent lumps. Add to mushrooms along with next five ingredients. Mix well. Arrange chicken in a 9-inch by 9-inch baking pan that has been sprayed with non-stick coating. Pour sauce over chicken and sprinkle with paprika. Cover with wax paper and cook at 50% power for 14 - 20 minutes, rotating 1/4 turn every 5 minutes and stirring sauce when rotating. This dish is done when sauce is thickened and chicken is no longer pink.

**Conventional Method:** Preheat oven to 350 degrees. Sauté mushrooms and onion in a skillet that has been sprayed with a non-stick coating. Shake flour with water to prevent lumps. Add to mushrooms along with next five ingredients. Cook, stirring constantly, until thickened. Arrange chicken in a 9-inch by 9-inch baking dish that has been sprayed with non-stick coating. Pour sauce over chicken and sprinkle with paprika. Bake for 30 minutes or until chicken is no longer pink.

Yield: 4 servings
One serving: 1/4 recipe
Calories per serving: 205
Exchanges*: 4 lean meat, 1 vegetable

*Due to the low fat content of chicken breasts, the calories are less than the exchanges compute.

# Chicken Breasts Supreme

This is a special way to serve chicken. It is so moist and flavorful.

**2 lbs. boneless, skinless chicken breasts**
**1/2 cup Homemade Breading (page 62)**
**1/2 cup sliced onion**
**1/2 cup Swanson's chicken broth (30%), fat removed**
**1/2 cup dry white wine or vermouth**
**2 cups mushrooms, sliced**

Preheat oven to 375 degrees. Coat chicken with breading and arrange in a 9-inch by 13-inch baking pan that has been sprayed with non-stick coating. Spray skillet with non-stick coating and sauté onions. Add broth and wine and bring to a boil. Pour around chicken. Bake, uncovered, 30 minutes. Meanwhile, sauté mushrooms in a skillet that has been sprayed with non-stick coating. Arrange around chicken after the chicken has cooked for 30 minutes. Bake an additional 10 minutes or until chicken is no longer pink.

Yield: 8 servings
One serving: 1/8 of recipe
Calories per serving: 190
Exchanges*: 4 lean meat, 1/2 starch

*Due to the low fat content of chicken breasts, the calories are less than the exchanges would compute.

# Chicken Cacciatore

This has a delicious flavor and it is especially good when served with the Dumpling recipe in this book.

**1 1/2 lb. boneless, skinless chicken breasts or 2 1/2 lb.-3 lb. chicken parts (with bone), skin removed**
**1 can (16 oz.) stewed tomatoes***
**1 onion, sliced**
**1 tsp. Italian herb seasoning**
**1 can (8 oz.) tomato sauce***
**2 cups frozen peas**

Spray a large saucepan with non-stick coating. Add chicken and remaining ingredients, except peas. Cover and simmer, stirring occasionally, for 25-35 minutes. Add peas and cook for 10 minutes.

Top with dumplings (optional).

Yield: 6 servings
One serving: 1/6 recipe
Calories per serving: 230
Exchanges**: 4 lean meat, 1 vegetable, 1/2 starch

*Sodium is figured for canned without salt.

**Due to the low fat content of chicken breasts, the calories are less than the exchanges compute.

Variation: Substitute canned string beans for peas. Add during the last 5 minutes of cooking.

# Chicken in Gravy

This makes a very good mushroom gravy that tastes great on rice or noodles. See Nutrient Analysis to compare sodium using regular and salt free broth.

**1 1/2 lbs. skinless, boneless chicken breasts or 2 1/2 lbs.-3 lbs. chicken parts (with bone), skin removed**
**1 can (8 1/2 oz.) artichoke hearts, drained**
**1/4 lb. mushrooms,sliced**
**1/4 tsp. pepper**
**1/2 tsp. paprika**
**1 1/3 cups chicken broth (fat removed)**
**4 Tbl. flour**
**1/2 tsp. salt (optional)**
**1/3 cup dry sherry (optional)**
**1/4 tsp. rosemary**

Preheat oven to 350 degrees. Arrange chicken in a 9-inch by 13-inch baking pan that has been sprayed with non-stick coating. Arrange artichoke hearts and mushrooms between chicken pieces. Sprinkle pepper and paprika over chicken. In a covered container, shake flour with 1/3 cup of cold broth. In a saucepan, add flour/broth mixture, remaining broth, salt (optional), dry sherry (optional), and rosemary. Heat on medium, stirring constantly until thickened. Pour over chicken and bake for 40-50 minutes.

Yield: 6 servings
One serving: 1/6 recipe
Calories per serving: 190
Exchanges*: 4 lean meat, 1 vegetable

*Due to the low fat content of chicken breasts, the calories are less than the exchanges would compute.

# Chicken Nuggets

These are a favorite for children. Serve with the Oven Fried Potato recipe in this book.

**1 lb. boneless, skinless chicken breasts**
**1/2 cup Homemade Breading (page 62)**
**Assorted mustards (optional)-see below**

Cut chicken into bite size pieces. Place breading in a plastic bag and add a few pieces of chicken at a time. Shake to coat evenly.

**Microwave Method:** Spray non-stick coating on a 12-inch by 8-inch baking dish. Arrange chicken pieces so they are not touching. Cover with wax paper and cook on high for 6-8 minutes or until chicken is tender, rearranging twice during cooking time.

**Coventional Oven:** Preheat oven to 425 degrees. Spray a cookie sheet with non-stick coating. Arrange chicken pieces so that they are not touching. Bake for 12-14 minutes.

Yield: 4 servings
One serving: 1/4 recipe
Calories per serving: 205
Exchanges*: 4 lean meat, 1 starch

*Due to the low fat content of chicken breasts, the calories are less than the exchanges would compute.

Optional mustards for dipping:
  Kraft SauceWorks Sweet'n Sour (25 Calories per Tablespoon)
  Old Spice Honey Mustard (35 Calories per Tablespoon)
  Colman's Hot English Mustard (prepared) or Colman's Mustard (dry)-follow package directions to mix with water (10 Calories per Tablespoon)

# Crispy Potato Chicken

If you like hash browns, you'll like this dish.

**1  medium potato, not peeled (5 oz.)**
**2 Tbl. Dijon mustard**
**1/2 tsp.chopped garlic**
**1 lb. boneless, skinless chicken breasts**
**1 tsp. oil (canola or olive)**
**1 tsp. pepper**

Preheat oven to 425 degrees.  Arrange chicken in a 9" by 9" baking dish that has been sprayed with non-stick coating.  Mix mustard and garlic.  Spread over chicken. Scrub potato, grate and mix well with oil. Spread over chicken. Sprinkle with pepper.  Bake for 25 to 35 minutes until chicken is done and potatoes are golden.

Yield: 4 servings
One serving: 1/4 recipe
Calories per serving: 205
Exchanges*: 4 lean meat, 1/2 starch

*Due to the low fat content of chicken breasts, the calories are less than the exchanges would compute.

# French Glazed Chicken

The orange glaze adds color as well as flavor to the chicken  This same glaze is used in French Glazed Fish.

**1 lb. skinless, boneless chicken breasts**
**1/4 cup low calorie French dressing**
**2 Tbl. low sugar apricot jam**
**1 Tbl. dried onion**
**2 Tbl. water**

Arrange chicken in a 9-inch by 9-inch pan that has been sprayed with non-stick coating.  Follow directions below for microwave or conventional oven.

**Conventional Oven:** Preheat oven to 350 degrees.  Bake, uncovered, for 20 minutes.  Mix remaining ingredients and spoon over chicken.  Return to oven for 10 minutes or until chicken is done and glaze is heated.

**Microwave Method:** Cover with plastic wrap, venting one corner.  Cook on high for 6-8 minutes, depending on thickness of chicken.  Rotate 1/4 turn halfway through cooking.  Drain any liquid.  Mix remaining ingredients and spoon over chicken.  Cook for 1-2 minutes or until glaze is heated.

Yield: 4 servings
One serving: 1/4 recipe
Calories per serving: 190
Exchanges*: 4 lean meat, 1 vegetable

*Due to the low fat content of chicken breasts, the calories are less than the exchanges would compute.

# Oven Fried Chicken

This is a good alternative to traditional fried chicken. Serve it with baked potatoes or the Oven Fried Potato recipe in this book.

**1 1/2 lbs. boneless, skinless chicken breasts or 2 1/2 lbs.- 3lbs. chicken parts (with bone), skin removed**
**4 Tbl. Homemade Breading (see page 62)**

Preheat oven to 425 degrees. Place breading in a plastic bag and shake a few pieces of chicken in the breading. Arrange chicken pieces so that they are not touching in a 9-inch by 13-inch baking dish that has been sprayed with non-stick coating. Bake boneless chicken breasts for 15-20 minutes and chicken parts for 45 to 60 minutes.

Yield: 6 servings
One serving: 1/6 recipe
Calories per serving: 170
Exchanges*: 4 lean meat, 1/4 starch

*Due to the low fat content of chicken breasts, the calories are less than the exchanges would compute.

# Chicken Polynesian

Two versions of preparation are listed here. The first one takes longer to cook but has a sauce that is especially good on rice. The second version is prepared without the sauce, uses less sugar, and cooks in only 30 minutes.

**2 lbs. boneless, skinless chicken breasts or 3 1/2 lbs.-4 lb. chicken parts, (with bone)**
**1/4 cup soy sauce**
**1/4 cup water**
**1/2 cup white wine (broth may be substituted)**
**2 tsp. liquid smoke**
**1 tsp. ginger**
**1/4 -1/2 cup brown sugar***
**1-2 tsp. dry mustard**

**Sauce Version:** Skin chicken. Mix next five ingredients in a 9-inch by 13-inch baking pan. Marinate chicken pieces for 1- 2 hours, turning the pieces halfway through the marinating time. Preheat oven to 350 degrees. Leave chicken in the marinade. Top chicken pieces with 1/2 cup brown sugar and mustard. Bake for 40-50 minutes, basting during the last 15 minutes of cooking time.

**Quick Version:** Skin chicken. Mix next five ingredients and marinate chicken for 1-2 hours, turning pieces halfway through the marinating time. Drain marinade. Preheat oven to 350 degrees. Spray a 9-inch by 13-inch baking pan with non-stick cooking spray. Arrange chicken in pan and top with 1/4 cup brown sugar and mustard. Bake for 30 minutes.

Yield: 8 servings
One serving: 1/8 recipe
Calories per serving : 210-Sauce Version, 185-Quick Version
Exchanges**: 4 lean meat, 1 starch-Sauce Version
                  4 lean meat, 1/2 starch-Quick Version

*People with diabetes should use a brown sugar substitute. Calories would be 160 and the exchange would be 4 lean meat.

**Due to the low fat content of chicken breasts, calories are less than the exchanges would compute.

# Rolled Chicken and Asparagus

This attractive dish is so easy to assemble and yet looks so impressive. It is good served hot or cold.

**1 lb. boneless, skinless chicken breasts**
**24 to 30 asparagus spears (tough ends removed)**
**2 Tbl. lemon juice**
**6 green onions, chopped**
**1/2 tsp. salt (optional)**
**1/2 tsp. pepper**

Preheat oven to 350 degrees. Cut chicken breasts into 8 or 10 strips, each about 1-inch by 5-inches long. Wrap each strip in a corkscrew fashion around 2 or 3 uncooked asparagus spears. Fasten with toothpicks. Place in a covered baking dish that has been sprayed with a non-stick coating. Sprinkle with lemon juice, green onions, salt (optional), and pepper. Cover and bake 25 to 30 minutes. Remove toothpicks. Serve hot or refrigerate until chilled and serve cold.

Yield: 4 servings
One serving: 1/4 recipe
Calories per serving: 180
Exchanges*: 4 lean meat, 1 vegetable

*Due to the low fat content of chicken breasts, the calories are less than the exchanges would compute.

# Sweet and Sour Chicken

Serve this recipe over rice or noodles.

**1 can (8 oz.) unsweetened pineapple chunks, packed in juice**
**1 lb. boneless, skinless chicken breasts**
**1 cup Swanson's chicken broth (30% less salt)**
**1/4 cup vinegar**
**1/4 cup brown sugar or artificial sweetener***
**2 tsp. soy sauce**
**1/2 tsp. chopped garlic**
**1 cup sliced celery**
**1 small onion, quartered**
**1 green pepper, sliced**
**3 Tbl. cornstarch**
**1/4 cup water**

Drain pineapple, reserving the juice. Cut chicken into bite size pieces and place in a saucepan. Add reserved juice, broth, vinegar, brown sugar, soy sauce, and garlic. Cover and simmer over low heat for 15 minutes. Add vegetables and pineapple. Cook 10 minutes, stirring occasionally. Combine cornstarch and water. Gradually stir into hot mixture. Continue to cook until thickened, stirring constantly. Serve with quick cooking brown rice.

Yield: about 5 cups (5 servings)
One serving: 1 cup
Calories per serving: 230 with sugar; 190 with Equal
Exchanges**:  with sugar: 3 lean meat, 1 starch, 1 vegetable, 1/2 fruit
            with Equal: reduce starch to 1/2

*If using Equal, add 5-6 packets after mixture is thickened with cornstarch.

**Due to the low fat content of chicken breasts, the calories are less than the exchanges would compute.

# Yogurt Cumin Chicken

The combination of cumin, yogurt and jam makes this a flavorful dish.

**1 lb. boneless, skinless chicken breasts**
**1/3 cup plain nonfat yogurt**
**3 Tbl. low sugar apricot jam**
**1 tsp. cumin**
**1/2 tsp. salt (optional)**

**Conventional Oven:** Preheat oven to 350 degrees. Arrange chicken in a pan that has been sprayed with non-stick coating. Bake, uncovered, for 20 minutes. Mix remaining ingredients and spoon over chicken. Bake for 10 minutes or until chicken is no longer pink and sauce is heated.

**Microwave Method:** Cover with plastic wrap, venting one corner. Cook on high for 6-8 minutes, depending on thickness of chicken, rotating 1/4 turn halfway through cooking time. Drain any liquid. Mix remaining ingredients and spoon over chicken. Cook for 1-2 minutes or until sauce is heated.

**Broiler or Barbecue Method:** Cut 3 shallow slits length-wise in each chicken breast half. Place slit side down on broiler pan. Mix remaining ingredients. Spoon half on chicken. Broil 3-4 inches from heat for 4 minutes. Turn chicken over and spoon on remaining yogurt mixture. Broil 5 minutes longer or until chicken is no longer pink.

Yield: 4 servings
One serving: 1/4 recipe
Calories per serving: 180
Exchanges*: 4 lean meat, 1/3 fruit

*Due to the low fat content of chicken breasts, the calories are less than the exchanges would compute.

# Sausage and Sauerkraut

This quick meal uses turkey sausage instead of the traditional Polish keilbasa. It is available in many grocery stores. The sodium from the sauerkraut is significantly reduced by rinsing it twice, however, it can be reduced further by substituting cabbage (see variation below). This recipe is still high in sodium, due to the sausage, and should be limited.

**1 jar (32 oz.) sauerkraut**
**1 lb. turkey smoked sausage**
**2 cups unpeeled potatoes, thinly sliced**
**1/2 cup onion, thinly sliced**

**Conventional Oven:** Preheat oven to 350 degrees. Drain sauerkraut. Add water and drain. Add water and drain again. Place in a large casserole. Top with onions and potatoes. Cut sausage into serving pieces (about 10) and place on top. Cover and cook for 1 hour or until potatoes are tender.

**Microwave Method:** Cook potatoes and onions on high for 5 minutes, stirring once halfway through cooking time. Drain sauerkraut. Add water and drain. Add water and drain again. Top potatoes with sauerkraut. Cut sausage into serving size pieces (about 10). Place over sauerkraut. Cover and microwave on high for 7 minutes, rearranging halfway through cooking time.

Yield: about 8 cups (5 servings)
One serving: 1/5 recipe
Calories per serving: 210
Exchanges: 2 lean meat, 1 vegetable, 1 starch

Variation: Substitute shredded cabbage for all or part of the sauerkraut. Cook with potatoes, before adding sausage, when using the microwave.

# Seafood

It is much too easy to overcook fish. The general rule is to cook ten minutes for each inch of thickness. Fish should be cooked until opaque and should flake easily with a fork. Some of my favorites are halibut, orange roughy, cod, and fillet of sole.

The quality of frozen fish is usually very good as it is often frozen within four hours of being caught. Fresh fish sold in grocery stores may be as many as ten days old. Find out when fresh fish arrives in your supermarket. You can usually count on good quality if it is cooked within two days after it arrives at the grocery store. Look for frozen cooked shrimp in place of canned. It has much better flavor and is lower in sodium.

Many of the fish recipes have a notation stating that the calories are less than the *Exchanges* would compute. This is because red snapper was used in the analysis and it has about one half of a gram of fat per ounce instead of the three grams of fat used in the *Exchange List* for the lean meat group.

# Oven Fried Fish

This is a good substitute for fried fish since it eliminates the oil. Serve with the Fresh Cucumber Sauce recipe in this book.

**1 lb. fish fillets (snapper, sole)**
**1/4 cup Homemade Breading (page 62)**

Preheat oven to 450 degrees. Spray baking sheet with non-stick coating. Cut fish into serving size pieces. Coat fish with breading. Bake for 10 minutes, per inch of thickness, or until fish flakes easily.

Yield: 4 servings
One serving : 1/4 recipe
Calories per serving: 135
Exchanges*: 3 lean meat, 1/3 starch

*Due to the low fat content of fish, the calories are less than the exchanges would compute.

# Oven Fried Oysters

I use the extra small oysters and serve them with seafood cocktail sauce or the Fresh Cucumber Sauce recipe in this book.

**1 jar (16 oz.) oysters, drained**
**1/2 cup Homemade Breading (page 62)**

Preheat oven to 425 degrees. Spray a baking sheet with non-stick coating. Place breading mix in a plastic bag. Place oysters in bag, a few at a time, and shake to coat. Arrange on baking sheet so oysters are not touching. Bake for 10-15 minutes, depending on the size of the oysters.

Yield: 4 servings
One Serving: 1/4 recipe
Calories per serving: 125
Exchanges: 1 lean meat, 1 starch

# Clam Fettucini

This recipe uses staple foods that I keep stocked in my cupboard. It's quick to put together and it is also one of my childrens' favorite dishes. Serve topped with a sprinkle of Parmesan cheese.

**12 oz. uncooked fettucini noodles (eggless)**
**3 cans (6.5 oz. each) minced clams, undrained**
**3 tsp. chopped garlic**
**1/2 tsp. dried thyme**
**1 Tbl. lemon juice**
**1/4 tsp. salt (optional)**

Cook noodles according to package directions. Drain. Return to pan and add remaining ingredients. Heat thoroughly. Turn off heat. Cover and let sit until liquid is absorbed or if you prefer more moisture, serve immediately.

Yield: about 7 cups (7 servings)
One serving: 1 cup
Calories per serving: 225
Exchanges: 2 starch, 1 lean meat

# Crab Delight

This recipe can be served hot or cold. It's quick to put together and is a good way to combine vegetables with seafood.  Use fresh crab to lower the sodium.

**8 oz. imitation or fresh crab**
**1 package (10 oz.) frozen Oriental Style vegetables**
**1/4 tsp. garlic powder**
**1/4 tsp. ground ginger**
**1 can (8oz.) sliced water chestnuts, drained**
**2 tsp. soy sauce (optional)**

Combine crab, vegetables, and seasonings.  Heat according to directions on package for cooking vegetables.  Add soy sauce, water chestnuts and heat thoroughly.

Yield: about 4 cups (4 servings)
One serving: 1 cup
Calories per serving: 100
Exchanges: 1 lean meat, 2 vegetables

# Salmon Cakes

This recipe is especially good with fresh red pepper but a jar of pimentos will do. Leftover salmon is good to use and it is much lower in sodium than the canned red salmon. The taste of Miracle Whip adds a touch of sweetness which is preferred over the mayonnaise taste.

**1 can (15 1/2 oz.) red salmon, drained (or 2 cups flaked)**
**1 tsp. onion powder**
**1/4 cup diced red pepper or canned pimento (2 oz. jar)**
**6 saltines (unsalted top), crushed**
**3 Tbl. Miracle Whip Light**
**1 tsp. lemon juice**
**4 drops Tabasco sauce**

Remove skin from fish. Combine all ingredients in a medium bowl, mashing salmon bones with a fork. Shape into 4 cakes. Spray a skillet with non-stick cooking spray, and heat over medium heat. Cook salmon cakes, turning once, until lightly browned on each side.

Yield: 4 servings
One serving: 1 cake
Calories per serving: 250
Exchanges: 3 medium fat meat, 1/3 starch

# Baked Fish with Bottled Toppings

There are many bottled toppings that can be added to fish during the last few minutes of cooking. They add variety and convenience. Keep several of these on hand. Some of these may be high in sodium, but you can significantly reduce the sodium by using less.

**1 lb. fish fillets (snapper, sole)**
**1/4 cup of one of the following bottled toppings:**
  **S & W Mesquite Cooking Sauce & Marinade**
  **Lea & Perrins White Worcestershire Sauce**
  **Kraft Sauceworks Sweet'n Sour Sauce**
  **Ragu 100% Natural Pizza Sauce**
  **Old Spice Honey Mustard**
  **Milani 1890 Dill Sauce**
  **Lime Juice**

Arrange fish in a 9-inch by 13-inch baking pan that has been sprayed with non-stick coating. Follow directions below for microwave or conventional oven.

**Oven Method:** Preheat oven to 450 degrees. Bake, uncovered, for 4-5 minutes per half inch thickness of fish. Drain any liquid. Top fillets with 1/4 cup of one of the above toppings. Bake for 2 minutes to heat sauce.

**Microwave Method:** Cover with plastic wrap, venting one corner. Cook on high for 4-6 minutes, depending on thickness of fish. Rotate 1/4 turn halfway through cooking. Drain any liquid. Top fillets with 1/4 cup of one of the above toppings. Cook for 1-2 minutes or until sauce is heated.

Yield: 4 servings
One serving: 1/4 the recipe
Calories for fish: 110
Exchange*: 3 lean meat

*Due to the low fat content of fish, the calories are less than the exchanges would compute.

# CALORIES AND EXCHANGES FOR 1 TBL. OF THE FOLLOWING:

**Lea & Perrins White Wine Worcestershire Sauce**
Calories: 9      Exchange: "free"

**Kraft Sauceworks Sweet'n Sour Sauce**
Calories: 25      Exchange: 1/2 fruit

**Ragu 100% Natural Pizza Sauce**
Calories: 8      Exchange: "free"

**Old Spice Honey Mustard**
Calories: 35      Exchange: 1/2 fruit

**Milani 1890 Dill Sauce**
Calories: 1      Exchange: "free"

**Lime Juice**
Calories: 4      Exchange: "free"

Nutrition information was not available for **S &W Mesquite Cooking Sauce & Marinade.**

# Fillets of Sole Thermidor

This is a good recipe to serve for company. Adding shrimp or crab (see variation below) makes this a very special dish.

**2 lbs. fillets of sole**
**1 tsp. Molly McButter**
**3/4 cup skim milk (divided)**
**2 Tbl. cornstarch**
**2 oz. grated, low fat cheese**
**3 Tbl. dry sherry**
**dash of paprika**

Preheat oven to 350 degrees. Sprinkle fish fillets with Molly McButter. Roll up each fillet and place seam side down in a baking dish. Pour 1/4 cup milk over fillets. Cover and bake for 25 minutes, or until fish flakes easily. Mix 1/2 cup milk with cornstarch and microwave on high for 50 seconds, stirring once (or cook in saucepan until thickened). Stir in cheese and sherry. Microwave for 20 seconds more (or heat in saucepan until all ingredients are blended). Drain liquid from fish, discarding all but 1/2 cup. Add 1/2 cup of fish liquid to sauce. Pour over fish and sprinkle with paprika.

Yield: 8 servings
One serving: 1/8 the recipe
Calories per serving: 150
Exchanges*: 3 1/2 lean meat

Variation: Fill each fillet with a tablespoon of shrimp or crab before rolling up. Also add 1/2 cup shrimp or crab to sauce. Imitation crab works well.

*Due to the low fat content of fish, the calories are less than the exchanges would compute.

# Fish in Salsa

This is a favorite for salsa lovers. Bottled salsa or the salsa recipe in this book can be used. Sodium is figured for bottled salsa. To reduce the sodium, use the salsa recipe in this book.

**1 lb. fish fillets (snapper, sole)**
**3/4 cup salsa**

Arrange fish in a 9-inch by 13-inch pan that has been sprayed with non-stick coating. Follow directions below for microwave or conventional oven.

**Conventional Oven:** Preheat oven to 450 degrees. Bake, uncovered, for 4-6 minutes per 1/2 inch thickness. Drain any liquid. Spoon salsa over fish. Return to oven for 2 minutes to heat salsa.

**Microwave Method:** Cover with plastic wrap, venting one corner. Cook on high for 4-6 minutes, depending on thickness of fish. Rotate 1/4 turn halfway through cooking. Drain any liquid. Spoon salsa over fish. Cook for 1-2 minutes or until salsa is heated.

Yield: 4 servings
One serving: 1/4 recipe
Calories per serving: 130
Exchanges*: 3 lean meat, 1 vegetable

*Due to the low fat content of fish, the calories are less than the exchanges would compute.

# French Glazed Fish

The orange glaze adds color as well as flavor to the fish. This same glaze is used in French Glazed Chicken.

**1 lb. fish fillets (snapper, sole)**
**1/4 cup low calorie French dressing**
**2 Tbl. low sugar apricot jam**
**1 Tbl. minced dried onion**
**2 Tbl. water**

Arrange fish in a 9-inch by 13-inch baking pan that has been sprayed with non-stick coating. Follow directions for microwave or conventional oven below.

**Conventional Oven:** Preheat oven to 450 degrees. Bake, uncovered, for 4-5 minutes per half inch thickness of fish. Drain any liquid. Combine remaining ingredients and spoon over fish. Return to oven for 2 minutes to heat sauce.

**Microwave Method:** Cover with plastic wrap, venting one corner. Cook on high for 4-6 minutes, depending on thickness of fish. Rotate 1/4 turn halfway through cooking time. Drain any liquid. Mix remaining ingredients and spoon over fish. Cook for 1-2 minutes or until sauce is heated.

Yield: 4 servings
One serving: 1/4 recipe
Calories per serving: 150
Exchanges*: 3 lean meat, 1/2 fruit

*Due to the low fat content of fish, the calories are less than the exchanges would compute.

# Lemon Fish

This has a very good flavor and is so easy to prepare.

**1 lb. fish fillets (snapper, sole)**
**1/4 cup white wine or chicken broth**
**4-6 lemon slices**
**1/2 tsp. Molly McButter**
**1/8 tsp. pepper**
**1 Tbl. dried parsley**

Arrange fish in a 9-inch by 13-inch baking pan. Top with remaining ingredients. Follow directions below for microwave or conventional oven.

**Microwave Method:** Cover with plastic wrap, venting one corner. Cook on high for 5-8 minutes (depending on thickness), rotating 1/4 turn halfway through cooking. Fish is done when it flakes easily with a fork.

**Conventional Oven:** Preheat oven to 450 degrees. Bake fish, uncovered, for 10 minutes per inch of thickness, or until fish flakes easily with a fork.

Yield: 4 servings
One serving: 1/4 recipe
Calories per serving: 120
Exchanges*: 3 lean meat

*Due to the low fat content of fish, the calories are less than the exchanges would compute.

## Poached Fish

This quick method for cooking fish also adds a good flavor.

**1 lb. fish fillets (snapper, sole)**
**1 cup Swanson's chicken broth (30% less salt), fat removed**
**2 Tbl. lemon juice**
**1/4 tsp. pepper**
**2 bay leaves**
**1/2 tsp. chopped garlic**
**2 Tbl. dry sherry (optional)**

In a large skillet, mix everything except fish. Bring to a boil. Reduce heat and add fish. Simmer, covered, for 3-5 minutes, depending on thickness, or until fish flakes easily. Remove fish with slotted spatula.

Yield: 4 servings
One serving: 1/4 recipe
Calories per serving: 110
Exchanges*: 3 lean meat

*Due to the low fat content of fish, the calories are less than the exchanges would compute.

# Spanish Baked Fish

This quick dish has a good flavor.

**1 lbs. fish fillets (snapper or sole)**
**1 can (8 oz.) tomato sauce***
**1/2 tsp. chopped garlic**
**1/2 cup sliced onions**
**1/2 tsp. chili powder**
**1/4 tsp. oregano**
**1/4 tsp. cumin**

Preheat oven to 450 degrees. Arrange fish in a baking dish that has been sprayed with non-stick coating. Mix remaining ingredients and pour over fish. Bake for 10-20 minutes or until fish flakes easily.

Yield: 4 servings
One serving: 1/4 recipe
Calories per serving: 140
Exchanges**: 3 lean meat, 1 vegetable

*Sodium is figured for unsalted.

**Due to the low fat content of fish, the calories are lower than the exchanges would compute.

# Sweet Mustard Fish

This sauce has an interesting taste that adds variety to fish meals. Sodium is figured for bottled salsa. To reduce the sodium, prepare the salsa recipe in this book.

**1 lb. fish fillets (snapper, sole)**
**1/2 cup salsa, thick and chunky**
**2 Tbl. honey***
**2 Tbl. Dijon mustard**

Arrange fish in a 9-inch by 13-inch pan that has been sprayed with non-stick coating. Follow directions below for microwave or conventional oven.

**Conventional Oven:** Preheat oven to 450 degrees. Bake, uncovered, for 4-6 minutes per 1/2 inch thickness of fish. Drain any liquid. Combine remaining ingredients and spoon over fish. Return to oven for 2 minutes to heat sauce.

**Microwave Method:** Cover with plastic wrap, venting one corner. Cook on high for 4-6 minutes, depending on thickness of fish. Rotate 1/4 turn halfway through cooking. Drain any liquid. Mix remaining ingredients and pour over fish. Cook for 1-2 minutes or until sauce is heated.

Yield: 4 servings
One serving: 1/4 recipe
Calories per serving: 165
Exchanges**: 3 lean meat, 3/4 starch

*People with diabetes should substitute 2-3 pkts. of Equal for the honey. Calories will be reduced to 140 and the starch reduced to 1/3.

**Due to the low fat content of fish, the calories are less than the exchanges would compute.

# Tarragon Fish

This recipe has a distinct tarragon flavor and is another easy way to add variety to fish meals.

**1 lbs. fish fillets (snapper, sole)**
**1/2 cup plain nonfat yogurt**
**1 tsp. dried tarragon**
**1 oz. grated part skim mozzarella cheese**

Arrange fish in a 9-inch by 13-inch pan that has been sprayed with non-stick coating. Follow directions below for microwave or conventional oven.

**Conventional Oven:** Preheat oven to 450 degrees. Bake, uncovered, for 4-6 minutes per 1/2 inch thickness of fish. Drain any liquid. Mix remaining ingredients and spread over fish. Bake 2 minutes or until cheese is melted.

**Microwave Method:** Cover with plastic wrap, venting one corner. Cook on high for 4-6 minutes, depending on thickness of fish. Rotate 1/4 turn halfway through cooking. Drain any liquid. Mix remaining ingredients and spread over fish. Cook for 1-2 minutes or until cheese is melted.

Yield: 4 servings
One serving: 1/4 recipe
Calories per serving: 145
Exchanges*: 3 1/2 lean meat

*Due to the low fat content of fish, the calories are less than the exchanges would compute.

# Yogurt Cumin Fish

This is a delicious way to serve fish when you're in a hurry. I like the combination of cumin with the sweetness of jam.

**1 lb. fish fillets (snapper, sole)**
**1/3 cup plain nonfat yogurt**
**3 Tbl. low sugar apricot jam**
**1 tsp. cumin**
**1/2 tsp. salt (optional)**

Arrange fish in a 9-inch by 13-inch baking pan that has been sprayed with non-stick coating. Follow directions below for microwave or conventional oven.

**Oven Method:** Preheat oven to 450 degrees. Bake, uncovered, for 4-5 minutes per half inch thickness of fish. Drain any liquid. Mix remaining ingredients and pour over fish. Bake for 2 minutes to heat sauce.

**Microwave Method:** Cover with plastic wrap, venting one corner. Cook on high for 4-6 minutes, depending on thickness of fish. Rotate 1/4 turn halway through cooking time. Drain any liquid. Mix remaining ingredients and pour over fish. Cook for 1-2 minutes or until sauce is heated.

Yield: 4 servings
One serving: 1/4 the recipe
Calories per serving: 140
Exchanges*: 3 lean meat, 1/3 fruit

*Due to the low fat content of fish, the calories are less than the exchanges would compute.

# SEAFOOD MARINADES

## Soy Marinade

This is my favorite fish marinade. It really gives a good flavor to seafood.

**1/4 cup oil (canola or olive)**
**3 Tbl. soy sauce**
**2 Tbl. water**
**1/4 cup white wine**
**1 tsp. chopped garlic**
**1/2 tsp. ginger**

Mix marinade ingredients and marinate fish for one to four hours in the refrigerator. Drain marinade and barbecue or broil fish until done.

Yield: 3/4 cup
Calories per 1/2 Tbl. : 25
Exchanges: 1/2 fat

## Lemon Basil Marinade

This is another flavorful marinade.

**2 Tbl. olive oil**
**1/4 cup. lemon juice**
**2 Tbl. finely chopped green onion**
**1/2 tsp. dried basil or 1 Tbl. fresh**
**1/4 tsp. salt (optional)**

Mix all ingredients. Marinate fish for one to four hours in the refrigerator. Drain marinade and broil or barbecue fish until done.

Yield: about 1/2 cup
Calories per 1 Tbl. : 15
Exchanges: "free"

eef & Pork

Include beef and pork for variety so you won't get tired of fish or chicken. Be sure to choose lean cuts such as top sirloin or tenderloin and trim off all visible fat. Broiling or barbecuing are good methods for cooking since the fat can drip out. Additional recipes are included in the *Ground Meat* section.

# Orange Pork Chops

This is a delicious and unusual way to serve pork chops.  It is a good dish for entertaining, especially if you use the outdoor barbecue.

**1/3 cup low sugar orange marmalade**
**2 Tbl. Dijon mustard**
**4  pork rib chops (cut 3 per pound)**
**4 bunches of green onions**

In a small saucepan mix marmalade and mustard.  Stir over medium heat until marmalade is melted.  Set aside.  Trim all fat from chops.  Place chops on rack of a broiler pan or use the outdoor barbecue.  Broil about 4 inches from the heat for 6 minutes.  Turn chops and broil for 2 more minutes.  Spoon half of the glaze over chops.   Broil 4 to 5 minutes more or until chops are no longer pink.  Meanwhile, slice onions diagonally into 1-inch pieces.  Spray a skillet with non-stick  coating  and  stir-fry  onions  2 minutes  or  until  crisp-tender.   Stir in remaining glaze and heat thoroughly.  Serve over chops.

Yield: 4 servings
One serving: 1/4 recipe
Calories per serving: 220
Exchanges: 3 lean meat, 2/3 fruit

# Chinese Barbecued Pork

This is as good as the barbecued pork you order as an appetizer in Chinese restaurants. You can also serve this as a main dish, or over boiled noodles.

**1 lb. boneless pork tenderloin (2 inches wide)**
**1/2 cup Roger Hong's Chinese Barbecue Sauce**
**Coleman's Mustard (dry) or Coleman's Hot English Mustard (prepared)**

Marinate pork in barbecue sauce overnight (or at least 4 hours). Preheat oven to 325 degrees. Discard marinade. Roast meat for 1 hour or until meat juices run clear. Slice 1/8 inch thick and refrigerate until serving.

To make hot mustard sauce from dry:

Mix 2 Tbl. of dry mustard with an equal amount of cold water. Stir until the consistency of thick cream. Allow to stand 10 minutes to develop full flavor.

To serve:  Dip pork in hot mustard sauce.

Yield: about 6 servings
One serving: 2 oz. pork
Calories per serving of pork: 105
Exchanges: 2 lean meat
Calories for 1 tsp. of mustard sauce: 10

# Pork Chop Suey

Using pork tenderloin eliminates the extra trimming of fat and bone.  It also makes this a quick and tasty dish.  If you like crisp vegetables, simmer for the lesser amount of time.

**1 lb. boneless pork tenderloin**
**1 Tbl. soy sauce**
**1/4 tsp. salt (optional)**
**1 cup beef broth, fat removed**
**1 cup sliced onion**
**2 cups sliced celery**
**2 1/2 Tbl. cornstarch**
**1/4 tsp. ginger**
**1 Tbl. molasses**
**1/4 cup water**
**1 can (16 oz.) bean sprouts, drained (or fresh)**

Cut pork into 1-inch strips, 1/4-inch thick.  Spray a large frying pan with non-stick cooking spray, and brown pork.  Add the next five ingredients, cover and simmer for 5-10 minutes.  Meanwhile, mix cornstarch, ginger, molasses, and water.  Stir into hot mixture and cook until thickened.  Add bean sprouts and heat thoroughly.  Serve over noodles or quick cooking brown rice.

Yield: about 5 cups (5 servings)
One serving: 1 cup
Calories per serving: 160
Exchanges:  2 1/2 lean meat, 1 vegetable

# Fajitas Barbecue Style

Marinate the meat all day for this tasty dish.

**1 lb. top sirloin steak, 1 inch thick**

**Marinade:**
**1/3 cup lime juice**
**1/4 tsp. salt (optional)**
**1/2 tsp. garlic powder**
**1/4 tsp. pepper**
**1 tsp. dried oregano**
**1 tsp. chili powder**

**8 flour tortillas, 6-inch size**
**1 cup each: shredded lettuce and chopped tomato**
**1/2 cup sliced green onion**
**1 oz. grated, low fat cheddar cheese**

Trim steak and place in a shallow bowl. Mix marinade ingredients and spread on both sides of steak. Refrigerate for 6-8 hours, turning halfway through marinating time. Drain marinade and discard. Broil or barbecue steak about 2-3 minutes on each side or until desired doneness. Carve crossgrain into thin slices. Heat tortillas in microwave or in a non-stick skillet. To serve, divide the meat, lettuce, tomato, onions, and cheese over 8 tortillas.

Yield: 8 filled tortillas (4 servings)
One serving: 2 filled tortillas
Calories per serving: 360
Exchanges: 3 1/2 lean meat, 2 starch

# Beef or Pork Fajitas

This is a quick dish that the entire family will enjoy.

**1 lb. boneless top sirloin or pork tenderloin**
**3 Tbl. lime juice**
**1/2 tsp. coriander**
**1/2 tsp. chili powder**
**1 green pepper, sliced**
**1 onion, sliced**
**8 flour tortillas (6 inch size)**
**salsa (optional)**

Cut meat into 1" strips. Mix lime juice with coriander and chili powder and pour over meat. Set aside for a few minutes or for up to three hours. Meanwhile, slice vegetables, add to meat mixture and stir. Spray a skillet with non-stick cooking spray and stir-fry meat and vegetables until done. Warm tortillas in microwave about 50 seconds on high or in non-stick skillet. Fill each tortilla with meat mixture and serve with salsa.

Yield: 8 filled tortillas (4 servings)
One serving: 2 filled torillas
Calories per serving: 325
Exchanges: 2 starch, 3 lean meat

# Chinese Pepper Steak

This is a family favorite that tastes great. If you like crisp vegetables, simmer for the lesser time.

**1 lb. boneless round steak, cut into thin strips**
**1 cup sliced or quartered onion**
**1 1/2 cups diagonally sliced celery**
**2 green peppers, sliced**
**1/2 tsp. salt (optional)**
**1 tsp. chopped garlic**
**1/2 tsp. pepper**
**1/2 tsp. sugar**
**2 cups beef broth, fat removed**
**4 Tbl. cornstarch**
**1/2 Tbl. soy sauce**
**1/2 cup water**

Spray a large skillet with a non-stick coating. Stir-fry beef strips until browned. Add all but the last three ingredients and simmer, covered, for 5-10 minutes. Meanwhile, mix cornstarch with soy sauce and water. Stir into hot mixture and continue cooking until thickened. Serve over noodles or quick cooking brown rice.

Yield: about 5 cups (5 servings)
One serving: 1 cup
Calories per serving: 200
Exchanges: 3 lean meat, 1 vegetable

# Stir-Fry

I use 4 to 5 cups of sliced vegetables in this recipe. If you use different vegetables each time you make this, it will seem like a new recipe.   Tougher vegetables should be added first for longer cooking and the more tender vegetables added last. Choose lean beef, pork, chicken, shrimp, or scallops to complete the dish. I prefer to cut the meat while it is partially frozen.

**1/2 lb. lean beef, pork, or chicken cut into 1/4 inch strips or 1/2 lb. of**
**scallops or shrimp**
**1 small onion, sliced**
**1 tsp. chopped garlic**
**2 cups fresh broccoli flowerets**
**1 cup  sliced carrots**
**1 cup  sliced mushrooms**
**1 tsp. soy sauce**
**2-4 Tbl. water**

Spray a skillet with non-stick coating.  Add meat or seafood and stir-fry with garlic until cooked.  Remove and keep warm.  Stir-fry carrots and onion until carrots are partially done.  Add water, as needed, to prevent sticking.  Add broccoli, mushrooms, and soy sauce. Stir-fry until vegetables are done to your liking.  Add meat or seafood.  Serve with rice or noodles.

Other vegetables that are good in stir-fry are: green or red peppers, celery, green onions, zucchini, cauliflower, cabbage, snow peas, bean sprouts.

Yield: 4 servings
One serving: 1/4 recipe
Calories per serving: beef or pork-150; chicken-135; shrimp-100
Exchanges: beef or pork: 2 lean meat, 2 vegetable
            chicken*: 2 lean meat, 2 vegetable
            shrimp: 1 lean meat, 2 vegetable

*Due to the low fat content of chicken, the calories are less than the exchanges would compute.

# Marinated Steak

This is a favorite marinade for steaks.  It really adds a good flavor.

**1 1/2 lbs.  boneless steak (round, flank,or top sirloin), well trimmed**

**Marinade:**
**1/3 cup soy sauce**
**1/3 cup chili sauce**
**1/4 cup water**
**1 Tbl. Worcestershire sauce**
**1/4 tsp. pepper**
**1/4 tsp. garlic powder**
**1/8 tsp. chili powder**
**1 Tbl. dried parsley**
**1 tsp. dried oregano**
**1/8 tsp. dry mustard**

Mix marinade ingredients in a container large enough to accommodate the steak.  Add steak, coating both sides with the mixture. Refrigerate and marinate for 2 to 4 hours, turning steak once halfway through the marinating time.  Drain marinade.  Barbecue or broil to desired doneness.

Yield: about 6 servings
One serving: 1/6 recipe
Calories per serving: 190
Exchanges: 3 1/2 lean meat

# Ground Meat Dishes

Ground beef, ground turkey, or ground venison or elk may be used in any of the recipes in this section. When buying ground beef, look for 9% fat or less. For ground turkey, look for 7 % fat. If you have wild meat butchered, be sure to specify that you do not want any fat added to the ground meat.

Using ground turkey will result in a lighter color. This is fine in chili or in other dishes where the meat is not so obvious. Your family may find it objectionable in other dishes such as meat loaf. However, the taste is good and worth a try.

Also, the *Cholesterol- Saturated Fat Index (CSI)* for ground turkey is less than it is for ground beef. This indicates that the cholesterol and saturated fat content of the turkey is preferable over the ground beef. Refer to the *Nutrient Analysis of Recipes* in the back of this book for the CSI for each recipe.

# Baked Meatballs

These are quick because you cook them in the oven. Make this large amount and freeze for convenience. These taste great in the recipes listed below.

**2 lbs. extra lean ground beef (9% fat or less)or ground turkey (7% fat)**
**1/2 cup egg substitute (equal to 2 eggs)**
**1 Tbl. dried parsley**
**1 cup oatmeal or cracker meal or oat bran**
**1 cup skim milk**
**1 tsp. salt (optional)**
**1/2 tsp. ground pepper**
**2 tsp. onion powder**
**1/4 tsp. nutmeg**

Preheat oven to 425 degrees. Mix all ingredients. Shape into 1 1/2 inch balls. Arrange on two baking sheets that have been sprayed with non-stick coating. Bake for 12 minutes or until done.

Yield: about 48 meatballs (16 servings)
One serving: 3 meatballs
Calories per serving: turkey-125; beef-135
Exchanges: 1 1/2 medium fat meat, 1/4 starch

Recipes used in: Swedish Meatballs
                 Meatball Sandwich
                 Spaghetti and Meatballs

# Spaghetti and Meatballs

This is an easy recipe if you have meatballs in the freezer and sauce in the cupboard. Complete the meal with a tossed salad.

**18 meatballs ( page 196)**
**1 jar (28 oz.) Ragu Homestyle Spaghetti Sauce (without meat)**
**3 cups cooked spaghetti noodles**

Heat meatballs in sauce. Serve over spaghetti noodles.

Yield: 6 servings
One serving: 1/2 cup sauce, 3 meatballs, and 1/2 cup noodles
Calories per serving: turkey-290; beef-305
Exchanges: 1 1/2 medium fat meat, 2 vegetable, 1 3/4 starch

# Swedish Meatballs

This is one of my families' favorite recipes. It tastes great with mashed potatoes, rice, or noodles. See Nutrient Analysis to compare sodium using regular broth, 30% less salt, and salt free broth.

**20 meatballs (page 196)**
**1 can (14 1/2 oz.) Swanson's beef broth or chicken 30% less salt)**
**3 1/2 Tbl. flour**

Remove fat from broth. Pour 1/4 of the broth in a covered container. Add flour and shake well to avoid lumps. In a sauce pan, combine remainder of broth with the flour mixture. Heat on medium, stirring constantly with a wire whip, until thickened. Add meatballs and heat thoroughly.

Yield: 5 servings
One serving: 1/5 recipe
Calories per serving: turkey-185; beef-205
Exchanges: 2 medium fat meat, 1/2 starch

Variation: Add one small can of drained mushrooms to the gravy when adding the meatballs.

# Meat Patties

I like these because they are so moist and have such a good flavor. You can also shape into a meatloaf instead of patties.

**1 lb. extra lean ground beef (9% fat or less) or ground turkey (7% fat)**
**1/4 cup egg substitute (equal to 1 egg)**
**1/2 Tbl. dried parsley**
**1/2 cup oatmeal or oatbran or cracker meal**
**1/2 cup skim milk**
**1 tsp. dry mustard**
**1/4 tsp. chopped garlic**
**1/2 tsp. salt (optional)**
**1/4 tsp. ground pepper**
**1 tsp. dried onion**

Mix all ingredients. Shape into 6 patties. Cook in the microwave, conventional oven, or on the barbecue.

**Conventional Oven:** Preheat oven to 425 degrees. Bake for 20 minutes.

**Microwave Oven:** Arrange in a circle, on a dish, leaving the center empty. Cover with wax paper and cook on high for 7-8 minutes, rotating 1/4 turn halfway through cooking time.

**Barbecue:** Cook over hot coals, turning once, until done.

Yield: 6 servings
One serving: 1/6 recipe
Calories per serving: turkey-165; beef-185
Exchanges: 2 medium fat meat, 1/4 starch

# Meat Loaf

The chopped vegetables add a good flavor to this meat loaf. However, if your children don't like to see vegetables in their meatloaf, use your blender and simply blend the vegetables with the milk (this also eliminates the chopping). Use the microwave method and have it ready in less that 30 minutes.

**1 1/2 lbs. extra lean ground beef (9% fat or less) or ground turkey (7% fat)**
**1/4 cup egg substitute (equal to 1 egg)**
**1/2 cup chopped onion**
**1/2 cup chopped green pepper**
**1 Tbl. dried parsley**
**3/4 cup finely chopped celery**
**3/4 cup oatmeal**
**3/4 cup skim milk**
**1/2 cup catsup**
**1 tsp. dry mustard**
**1/2 tsp. chopped garlic**
**1 tsp. salt (optional)**
**1/2 tsp. ground pepper**

**Conventional Oven:** Preheat oven to 325 degrees. Mix all ingredients. Shape into a loaf and bake for 1 hour.

**Microwave Oven:** Mix all ingredients. Pack lightly into a 10-inch glass dish, making a well in the center. Place empty glass, right side down, in center of dish. Cover with wax paper and cook on high for 18 minutes, rotating 1/4 turn after 6 minutes and again after another 6 minutes of cooking time. Let rest for 5 minutes before serving.

Yield: 8 servings
One serving: 1/8 recipe
Calories per serving: turkey-205; beef-230
Exchanges: 2 medium fat meat, 1 vegetable, 1/2 starch

# Pizza Meat Loaf

This is a family favorite that can be put together in a hurry. Serve with a salad and French bread.

**1 lb. extra lean ground beef (9% fat or less) or ground turkey (7% fat)**
**1/4 cup Ragu 100% Natural Pizza Sauce**
**1 oz. grated, part skim mozzarella cheese**
**1/2 cup thin sliced vegetables (green pepper and onion)**

**Conventional Oven:** Preheat oven to 425 degrees. Spray a 9-inch pie plate with a non-stick cooking spray. Pat the meat into a pie plate. Bake for 12-14 minutes. Drain any liquid. Top with pizza sauce, cheese, and vegetables. Return to oven for 5 minutes.

**Microwave Method:** Spray a 9-inch glass pie plate with non-stick coating. Pat the meat into the pie plate. Cover with wax paper and cook on high for 6 minutes turning 1/4 turn halfway through cooking time. Drain any liquid. Top with pizza sauce, cheese, and vegetables. Cook on high for 2 minutes until cheese is melted.

Yield: 4 servings
One serving: 1/4 pie
Calories per serving: turkey-220; beef-250
Exchanges: 3 medium fat meat, 1/2 vegetable

# Ground Meat, Cabbage, and Noodles

Sliced apples go well with this meal.

**1 1/4 cups water**
**1/3 cup Cream Soup Mix ( page 70)**
**6 oz. uncooked fettucini noodles (eggless)**
**1/2 lb. extra lean ground beef (9% fat or less) or ground turkey (7% fat)**
**1 medium onion, chopped**
**3/4 lb. cabbage, shredded**
**1/2 tsp. salt (optional)**
**1/8 tsp. pepper**

In a glass measuring cup, combine soup mix and water. Heat on high in micro-wave for 3-4 minutes, stirring several times until mixture thickens ( see page 70 for stovetop directions). Set aside. Cook noodles according to package directions and drain. Spray skillet with non-stick cooking spray and brown meat with onion. Remove meat and onion. Add cabbage to skillet and stir-fry until limp and tender. Add noodles, soup mixture, salt, pepper and meat to cabbage. Mix well.

Yield: about 7 cups (7servings)
One serving: 1 cup
Calories per serving: turkey-175; beef-185
Exchanges: 1 starch, 1 vegetable, 1 medium fat meat

Variation: Substitute sauerkraut for half of the cabbage.

# Sloppy Joes

Complete this meal by adding fresh fruit or a tossed salad.

**1 lb. extra lean ground beef (9% fat or less) or ground turkey (7% fat)**
**1/2 cup chopped onion**
**1 Tbl. prepared mustard**
**1 Tbl. catsup**
**1 can chicken gumbo soup**
**8 hamburger buns**

**Microwave Method:** Remove any fat from soup. Crumble meat, add onion, and cook on high in microwave for 4 minutes, turning halfway through cooking time. Add remaining ingredients and continue cooking for about 2 minutes or until heated thoroughly. Spoon 1/2 cup of mixture on 8 bun halves. Top with remaining buns.

**Stovetop Method:** Remove any fat from soup. Spray skillet with a non-stick cooking spray and brown meat and onion. Add remaining ingredients and simmer for about 10 minutes. Spoon 1/2 cup of mixture on 8 bun halves. Top with remaining buns.

For a crisp texture, bake at 475 degrees for 10 minutes before serving.

Yield: 3 1/2 to 4 cups mixture and 8 buns ( 8 servings)
One serving: 1 bun and 1/2 cup meat mixture
Calories per serving: turkey-240; beef-255
Exchanges: 1 1/2 medium fat meat, 1 1/2 starch, 1/2 vegetable

Variation: Decrease buns to 4. Spoon 1/2 cup meat mixture on each bun half and serve open face. Serving size would be 1/2 cup meat mixture and 1/2 bun. Calories are decreased by 60 and exchange is decreased to 3/4 starch.

# Moore

This is a quick dish that children can prepare.

**6 oz. uncooked fettucini noodles (eggless)**
**1 lb. extra lean ground beef (9% fat or less) or ground turkey (7% fat)**
**1/8 tsp. pepper**
**1 can (10 1/2 oz.) tomato soup**
**1 oz. grated, low fat cheddar cheese**

**Conventional method**: Cook fettucini as directed on package. Drain. Brown meat in a skillet that has been sprayed with a non-stick coating. Add cooked fettucini, pepper, and soup. Cook over low heat until hot. Top with cheese, cover and cook until cheese is melted.

**Microwave method:** Cook fettucini as directed on package. Drain. Crumble meat and cook in microwave on high. Stir at 1 1/2 minute intervals until done. Add fettucini, soup, and pepper. Cook on high for 3 minutes stirring after 1 1/2 minutes. Top with cheese and cook for 45 seconds or until cheese is melted.

Yield: about 5 cups (5 servings)
Serving size: 1 cup
Calories per serving: turkey-305; beef-330
Exchanges: 2 1/2 medium fat meat, 1 vegetable, 1 1/2 starch

# John Torrey

A friend doubles this recipe when she is entertaining a large group of people. It can be assembled in advance and refrigerated. Increase cooking time by 15 minutes if it has been refrigerated.

6 oz. uncooked elbow macaroni
1/2 lb. extra lean ground beef (9% fat or less) or ground turkey (7% fat)
1/2 green pepper, chopped
1 small onion, chopped
1 can (8 oz.) tomato sauce*
1 can (16 oz.) tomatoes*
2 oz. low fat cheddar cheese, cut into pieces
1/2 tsp. chopped garlic
1/4 tsp. salt (optional)
1/2 tsp. chili powder
1 can (4 oz.) chopped mushrooms, drained

Preheat oven to 350 degrees. Cook macaroni according to package directions. Drain. Spray skillet with a non-stick coating. Add ground beef, green pepper, and onion. Sauté until tender. Add remaining ingredients, including macaroni. Pour into a casserole dish that has been sprayed with non-stick coating. Bake, covered, for 35-40 minutes or until thoroughly heated.

Yield: about 7 cups (7 servings)
One serving: 1 cup
Calories per serving: turkey-210; beef-220
Exchanges: 1 medium fat meat, 1 1/2 starch, 1 vegetable

*Sodium is figured for canned without salt.

# Bean and Beef/Turkey Enchiladas

Children really like this recipe. I've listed two methods for assembling. Try the layered method if you are in a hurry.

**3/4 lb. extra lean ground beef (9% fat or less) or ground turkey (7% fat)**
**1 cup chopped onion**
**1 can (30 oz.) vegetarian refried breans**
**1 can (4 oz.) diced green chiles**
**1/2 tsp. cumin**
**1/2 tsp. chili powder**
**12 tortillas (6 inch size) flour or corn, cut into 1-inch strips**
**2 cans (10 oz. each) enchilada sauce**
**1/2 tsp. chopped garlic**
**4 oz. grated, low fat cheddar cheese**

Preheat oven to 375 degrees. Spray a large skillet with non-stick coating. Add onion and ground meat. Cook until meat is done. Add next four ingredients and mix well. Spray a 9-inch by 13-inch baking pan with non-stick coating. Add 1/4 tsp. garlic to each can of enchilada sauce. Pour 1/2 can of enchilada sauce in the bottom of the pan. Follow one of the methods below for rolling or layering. Bake for 20-25 minutes or until thoroughly heated. Top with cheese and return to oven for 5 minutes.

**Layered Method:** Follow this order: 1/3 of the tortilla strips, 1/2 of the bean mixture, 1/3 of tortillas, 1 can sauce, remainder of bean mixture, remainder of tortillas, remainder of sauce.

**Rolled Method:** Place filling in each tortilla. Roll to enclose. Place seam side down on baking dish. Pour remaining sauce over top.

Serving suggestion: Serve with salsa or Spanish Yogurt Dressing.

Yield: 12 servings
One serving: 1/12 recipe
Calories per serving: turkey-250; beef-260
Exchanges: 1 1/2 medium fat meat, 1 1/2 starch, 1 vegetable

# Ground Meat and Bean Casserole

This recipe is easy for children to prepare. Serve it with raw vegetable sticks or a salad.

**1 lb. extra lean ground beef (9% fat or less) or ground turkey (7% fat)**
**1/2 cup chopped onion**
**1 can (16 oz.) vegetarian baked beans**
**1/4 cup catsup**

**Stovetop Method:** Spray frying pan with a non-stick coating. Brown ground meat, add onion and cook until tender. Add remaining ingredients and heat thoroughly.

**Microwave Method:** Place crumbled ground meat and onion in a microwave safe dish. Cook on high for 4 minutes, stirring twice, turning halfway through cooking time. Add remaining ingredients and continue cooking for about 2 minutes, or until thoroughly heated.

Yield: about 4 cups
One serving: 1 cup
Calories per serving: turkey-215; beef-235
Exchanges: 2 medium fat meat, 1 starch

# Tortilla Pie

This makes a large amount so serve this for company or plan on having leftovers. Children really like this recipe.

2 lbs. extra lean ground beef (9% fat or less) or ground turkey (7% fat)
2 large onions, chopped
1 can (8oz.) tomato sauce*
1 jar (16 oz.) thick and chunky salsa
1 tsp. each: cumin, chili powder and garlic powder
1 can (17 oz.) creamed corn
12 corn tortillas, cut into 1-inch strips
2 oz. grated, part skim mozzarella cheese
2 oz. grated, low fat cheddar cheese

Preheat oven to 350 degrees. Spray a large skillet with non-stick coating. Brown meat with onion. Add sauces, seasonings, and corn. Mix well. Spray a 9-inch by 12-inch pan with non-stick coating. Layer mixture with tortillas, starting with one fourth of the meat mixture and topping with one third of the tortilla strips. Continue layering, ending with the meat mixture. Cover and bake for 35-40 minutes or until thoroughly heated. Add cheese and cook another 5 minutes.

Yield: 12 servings
One serving: 1/12 the recipe
Calories per serving: turkey-280; beef-300
Exchanges: 2 medium fat meat, 1 vegetable, 1 1/2 starch

*Sodium is figured for canned without salt.

# Desserts

The desserts in this section that are high in sugar are identified as being limited for people with diabetes. This means that occasional use may be appropriate but they should not be used on a daily basis.

# Cream Cheese Dessert

This light dessert tastes and looks so good.  It is especially attractive if layered in parfait glasses.  It is fairly high in sodium, so it should be limited.

**1 tub (12 oz.) Light Philadelphia Cream Cheese Product (room temperature)**
**1 large box (1.6 oz.) sugar-free vanilla instant pudding**
**3 cups skim milk**
**1 can (20 oz.) Lite Cherry Filling* (Wilderness brand)**

In a small mixing bowl, combine pudding mix and milk.  Beat on low speed to mix ingredients.  Add cream cheese.  Increase speed and beat until smooth and thickened.  Pour into individual or large serving dish.  Top with pie filling, and refrigerate.

Yield: 8 servings
One serving: 1/2 cup pudding mix
           1/4 cup filling
Calories per serving: 200
Exchanges: 1/2 milk, 1 starch, 1 1/2 fat

* The cherry filling contains sugar and should be limited by people with diabetes.

# Fruit Pizza For A Crowd*

I get lots of compliments when I make this because it looks so impressive. The secret is arranging the fruit in an attractive pattern. I often use a combination of strawberries, raspberries, blueberries, and kiwi fruit. Lite whipped topping can also be added. See notation below for using different size pans.

**1 package (20 oz.) Pillsbury's Best Sugar Cookie Dough**
**1 qt. strawberries, washed and hulled ( or other fresh fruit)**
**1 package (1.6 oz.) sugar-free vanilla instant pudding**
**3 cups skim milk**
**6 oz. (1/2 of a 12 oz. tub) Light Philadelphia Cream Cheese Product (room temperature)**

Preheat oven to 350 degrees. Spray a 16-inch pizza pan with a non-stick spray. Slice cookie dough into 1/4-inch thick slices. Arrange slices on pizza pan so that they are 1/2 to 1-inch apart. Bake for 18-20 minutes or until golden and set. Cool. In small mixing bowl, combine pudding mix and milk. Beat on low to mix. Add cream cheese and beat until smooth and thickened. Pour over cooled cookie crust. Arrange fruit on top.

Yield: 18 slices (18 servings)
One serving: 1/18 the pie
Calories per serving: 185
Exchanges: 1 1/2 starch, 1 1/2 fat

* People with diabetes should limit the use of this recipe because it contains significant amounts of sugar.

Note: This amount will also make four 8-inch pizzas or one 11-inch by 14-inch *and* an 8-inch pizza. 8-inch cake pans work fine.

# Fruit Slush

This is a low fat version of a "Blizzard." You can eat it with a spoon or increase the milk and drink it.

**1/2-3/4 cup frozen fruit (1/2 cup sliced, 3/4 cup whole berries)**
**1/2 cup skim milk, buttermilk or nonfat plain yogurt**
**1/4 tsp. vanilla extract**
**sweetener as needed: about 1-2 tsp. sugar or 1/2 to 1 pkt. Equal sweetener**

Blend first three ingredients until smooth. Sweeten to taste.

Yield: about 1 cup
One serving: 1 cup
Calories per serving: 95 with sugar; 80 with Equal
Exchanges: Using sugar: 1/2 milk, 3/4 fruit; Using Equal: 1/2 milk, 1/2 fruit

# Mock Plum Pudding

This rich tasting dessert was given to me by Claudia Schon. It had been served by her mother on special occasions. I changed the Jello to sugar-free and decreased the amount of nuts.

**1 box (0.3 oz.) sugar-free cherry Jello**
**1/2 cup raisins**
**1 box (8oz.) dates**
**1/4 cup chopped walnuts**
**1 cup Grapenuts cereal**
**1 tsp. cinnamon**
**1 tsp. nutmeg**

Mix Jello as directed on box. Add remaining ingredients and chill until firm, about 2 to 3 hours. Serve with lite whipped topping (optional).

Yield: about 3 cups (9 servings)
One serving: 1/3 cup
Calories per serving: 164
Exchanges: 2 fruit, 1/2 starch

# Apple Crisp*

This old fashioned dessert is good served warm or cold.

**4 cups peeled, sliced apples**
**1/4 cup water**
**4 tsp. firmly packed brown sugar**
**2 tsp. lemon juice**
**1 tsp. cinnamon**
**1/2 cups oats (quick or old fashioned)**
**1 Tbl. firmly packed brown sugar**
**1 Tbl. soft margarine**

Preheat oven to 375 degrees. Combine first 5 ingredients and mix well. Arrange apple mixture in an 8-inch by 8-inch baking dish that has been sprayed with non-stick coating. Combine remaining ingredients and sprinkle over apples. Bake for 30 minutes or until apples are tender and topping is lightly browned.

Yield: 8 servings
One serving: 1/8 recipe
Calories per serving: 80
Exchanges: 1/2 starch, 1/2 fruit

*This recipe contains 1 tsp. sugar per serving. People with diabetes may choose to use brown sugar substitute.

# Baked Apples

This microwave recipe has a good flavor because of the soda and spices. If you want a sweeter apple, sprinkle on a little Equal after cooking.

**4 small apples**
**1/3 cup diet raspberry soda**
**1/4 tsp. cinnamon**

Core apples, leaving 1/2 inch of bottom intact. Place in baking dish. Combine soda and cinnamon. Spoon into center of apples. Cover with plastic wrap and microwave on high for 4-6 minutes, rotating 1/4 turn after 2 minutes. Let stand 2 minutes before serving.

**Filling Variations:**

### Rum Baked Apples
**1/3 cup diet cream soda**
**1/2 tsp. rum extract**
**1/4 tsp. cinnamon**
**1/8 tsp. ginger**

### Maple Baked Apples
**1/3 cup diet cream soda**
**1/2 tsp. maple extract**
**1/4 tsp. nutmeg**
**1/4 tsp. allspice**

Yield: 4 servings
One serving: 1 apple
Calories per serving: 65
Exchanges: 1 fruit

# Apple Cake*

This moist cake is a family favorite. Serve it plain, with ice milk, or with lite whipped topping. Grate the apples in a food processor to save time.

**2/3 cup granulated sugar**
**1/2 cup brown sugar**
**1/4 cup vegetable oil (canola)**
**3 egg whites**
**2/3 cup unbleached flour**
**2/3 cup whole wheat flour**
**1/2 cup oat bran**
**1 1/2 tsp. baking soda**
**1 tsp. cinnamon**
**1/4 tsp. allspice**
**3 cups grated apples (unpeeled)**

Preheat oven to 350 degrees. In a large bowl, mix sugars, oil and egg whites until well blended. Add remaining ingredients, except apples, and stir just until moistened. Stir in apples. Pour into a 9-inch by 13-inch baking pan that has been sprayed with a non-stick coating. Bake for 25 to 30 minutes.

Yield: 16 servings
One serving: one piece, 2"x3"
Calories per serving: 145
Exchanges: 1 1/2 starch, 1/2 fat

*People with diabetes should limit the use of this recipe because it contains significant amounts of sugar.

# Chocolate Cake*

Chocolate lovers will really enjoy this moist, low fat cake. Serve plain or top with powdered sugar, lite whipped topping, or the Chocolate Glaze recipe in this book. If you prefer a smaller cake (8"x8"), halve all of the ingredients and bake for 25 minutes.

2 cups sugar
3 cups unbleached flour
1 tsp. salt (optional)
1/2 cup cocoa
2 tsp. baking soda
2 Tbl. vinegar
2/3 cup oil (canola)
2 tsp. vanilla extract
2 cups cold water

Preheat oven to 350 degrees. Mix first five ingredients. Add remainder of ingredients and mix until smooth. Pour into a 9-inch by 13-inch pan that has been sprayed with non-stick coating. Bake for 35-40 minutes. For cupcakes (makes about 24), bake for 20-25 minutes.

Yield: 16 servings (from 9-inch by 13-inch pan)
One serving: one piece, 2"x3"
Calories per serving: 265
Exchanges: 2 fat, 2 starch

*People with diabetes should limit use of this recipe because it contains significant amounts of sugar.

# Mandarin Orange Cake*

You may think I forgot the liquid, but I didn't. The oranges supply all the moisture needed.

1/2 cup sugar
1 cup unbleached flour
1/4 cup egg substitute (equal to 1 egg)
1 can (11 oz.) mandarin oranges, drained
1 tsp. baking soda
1/2 tsp. salt (optional)
2 Tbl. oil (canola)
1 tsp. vanilla

Preheat oven to 350 degrees. Mix all ingredients, mashing the oranges, and pour into a 9-inch by 9-inch pan that has been sprayed with non-stick coating. Bake for 30-35 minutes. Prepare topping (below).

Topping:
2 Tbl. firmly packed brown sugar
2 tsp. skim milk

Combine sugar and milk. In the microwave, heat on high until mixture starts to boil. Drizzle over hot cake.

Yield: 9 servings
One serving: 1 piece
Calories per serving: 140
Exchanges: 1 3/4 starch

* People with diabetes should limit the use of this recipe because it contains significant amounts of sugar.

# Pineapple Cake*

This very moist cake does not call for any kind of shortening. It's a great low fat choice that can be served plain, dusted with powdered sugar, or topped with lite whipped topping. Additional topping recipes are listed below.

**1 can (20 oz.) unsweetened crushed pineapple, in juice (undrained)**
**1/4 tsp. salt (optional)**
**2 cups unbleached flour**
**1 cup sugar**
**2 tsp. baking soda**
**1/2 cup egg substitute (equal to 2 eggs)**

Preheat oven to 350 degrees. Mix all ingredients and pour into a 9-inch by 13-inch pan that has been sprayed with non-stick coating. Bake for 30-35 minutes. Cool before adding a topping.

Optional topping recipes:  Cream Cheese Topping, page 227
                                          Orange Glaze, page 225

Yield: 16 servings
One serving: one piece, 2"x3"
Calories per serving: 130
Exchanges: 1 fruit, 1 starch


* People with diabetes should limit the use of this recipe because it contains significant amounts of sugar.

# Butterfly Cup Cakes*

My mother used to make these for school parties when I was a child. They are so special because each cup cake looks like it has a butterfly sitting on its' top. Chocolate fans can substitute chocolate cupcakes and fill with lite whipped topping.

**6 tsp. low sugar jam (strawberry or raspberry)**
**1 dz. cup cakes, yellow or white**
**1 box (0.9 oz.) sugar-free instant vanilla pudding mix**
**2 cups skim milk**
**powdered sugar (optional)**

Make pudding according to package directions, using skim milk. Let set for 5 minutes. Cut a cone shape from the top of each cup cake, according to diagram, and set aside. Fill cavity of each cup cake with 1 Tbl. pudding. Cut cones in half and place two halves, flat side down, on each cup cake to represent butterfly wings. Place 1/2 tsp. of jam in the center to resemble the body. Dust with powdered sugar (optional).

| Cut cone from top of cup cake. | Fill cavity with pudding. | Cut cone to represent wings. | Place "wings" on top. Add jam and dust with sugar. |

Yield: 12 servings (plus extra pudding)
One serving: 1 cup cake, 1 Tbl. pudding, 1/2 tsp. jam
Calories per serving: 125
Exchanges: 1 1/2 starch

* People with diabetes should limit the use of this recipe because it contains significant amounts of sugar.

# Fruit and Cake*

This is so easy and looks so attractive. I'll often serve this at a buffet or potluck. Store bought angel food cake, pound cake, or any cake in this book, will work well. Substitute different fresh fruit for variety. Dip apple, peach, and pear slices in lemon or pineapple juice to prevent browning.

**2 large bunches of grapes**
**1 cake (not frosted)**
**powdered sugar (optional)**

Wash and drain grapes. Slice cake into portions. Arrange slices down the center of an oval platter. Surround with bunches of grapes. Using a sifter, sprinkle powdered sugar over cake and grapes.

Yield: varies with cake
One serving: 10 grapes and 1 slice of angel food cake (1/12 of cake)
Calories per serving: 160
Exchanges: 1 fruit, 1 1/2 starch

* People with diabetes should limit the use of this recipe because it contains significant amounts of sugar.

# Sauce Topped Cake*

This can be assembled at a minute's notice and you can make it different each time by just varying the fruit and the sauce. Use fresh or canned fruit. I like pineapple slices with the Pina Colada Sauce. The Fruit Sauce recipe in this book can be substituted for the sauces listed.

**7 servings of cake (angel food or one listed in this book)**
**1 3/4 cups (one recipe) Pina Colada Sauce (page 225) or Liqueur Sauce (page 226)** *Note: both contain alcohol*
**3 1/2 cups fruit, sliced**

Arrange cake slices on individual plates. Top each with 1/2 cup of fruit, and 1/4 cup of sauce.

Yield: 7 servings
One serving: 1 slice of cake( 1/12 angel food), 1/2 cup of fruit, and 1/4 cup sauce
Calories per serving: 205
Exchanges: 1/2 fat, 1 fruit, 1 1/2 starch

* People with diabetes should limit the use of this recipe because it contains significant amounts of sugar. Both sauces listed contain alcohol and should not be used without consulting your physician.

# $S$weet Sauces, Glazes, & Toppings

These are easy ways to dress up a dessert. Several are very high in sugar and are not recommended for people with diabetes. However, the exchange is still listed so that you can figure it into your meal pattern should you choose to have it anyway.

# Cream Glaze*

Drizzle over cake or cupcakes just before serving.  Vary the flavor by using different extracts such as peppermint or rum.

**1/4 cup skim milk**
**1 cup powdered sugar**
**1/4 tsp. vanilla extract**

Mix ingredients.  Let sit for 5 minutes to dissolve sugar.

Yield: about 2/3 cup (16 servings)
One serving: 2 teaspoons
Calories per serving: 25
Exchanges: 1/2 fruit

* Not recommended for people with diabetes.

# Chocolate Glaze*

Drizzle this on chocolate cake just before serving.  It's very sweet, so a little goes a long way.

**1/4 cup skim milk**
**1 cup powdered sugar**
**1 Tbl. cocoa**
**1/4 tsp. vanilla extract**

Mix ingredients.  Let sit for 5 minutes to dissolve sugar.

Yield: about 2/3 cup (16 servings)
One serving: 2 teaspoons
Calories per serving: 25
Exchanges: 1/2 fruit

* Not recommended for people with diabetes.

# Orange Glaze*

This is another variation of the cream glaze.  It works well with the Pineapple Cake recipe in this book.

**1/4 cup orange juice**
**1 cup powdered sugar**

Mix ingredients.  Let sit for 5 minutes to dissolve sugar.

Yield: about 2/3 cup (16 servings)
One serving: 2 teaspoons
Calories per serving: 25
Exchanges: 1/2 fruit

\* Not recommended for people with diabetes.


# Pina Colada Sauce*

Serve this over cake, ice milk, or sliced fruit.  The combination with pineapple is especially good.  Adults only!

**1 1/2 cups nonfat pina colada yogurt (sweetened with Nutrasweet)**
**1/4 cup vodka**

Mix ingredients and refrigerate until serving.  This recipe is used in the Sauce Topped Cake recipe.

Yield: 1 3/4 cups (7 servings)
One serving: 1/4 cup
Calories per serving: 45
Exchanges: 1/4 milk; 1/2 fat

\*People with diabetes should consult their physician before using alcohol.

# Liqueur Sauce*

This can add a special touch when served over cake, ice milk, or sliced fruit.

**1 cup nonfat plain yogurt**
**1/4 cup orange juice concentrate**
**1/2 cup Triple Sec Liqueur or Grand Marnier Liqueur**

Mix all ingredients and refrigerate until serving. This recipe is used in the Sauce Topped Cake recipe.

Yield: 1 3/4 cups (7 servings)
One serving: 1/4 cup
Calories per serving: 80
Exchanges: 1 fruit, 1/2 fat

* People with diabetes should consult their physician before using alcohol.

# Fruit Sauce

Serve this when strawberries are in season. It's great on pancakes or as a topping on angel food cake.

**1 1/2 cups fresh raspberries or sliced strawberries or one 12 oz. package frozen raspberries or strawberries**
**2 packets Equal sweetener or 4 tsp. sugar**
**1 Tbl. lemon juice**

**Fresh fruit:** Place 1/2 cup of fruit in a blender with sweetener and lemon juice. Blend until smooth. Add remaining fruit and stir into mixture.

**Frozen fruit:** Thaw fruit. Place half of the fruit in blender with sweetener and lemon juice. Blend until smooth. Drain remaining fruit and stir into mixture.

Yield: 1 1/4 cups (5 servings)
One serving: 1/4 cup
Calories per serving: 25 with sugar; 15 with Equal
Exchanges: 1/2 fruit with sugar; 1/4 fruit with Equal

# Cream Cheese Topping

This isn't as sweet or rich as the traditional cream cheese frosting.   However, you'll find that a dollop tastes good on cake. For an attractive dessert, layer with sugar-free Jello or pudding in parfait glasses.

**1 small box (0.9 oz.) sugar-free vanilla instant pudding**
**2 cups skim milk**
**6 oz. (1/2 of a 12 oz.tub) Philadelphia Light Cream Cheese Product (room temperature)**

In a small mixing bowl combine pudding mix and milk.  Beat on low speed to mix well.  Add cream cheese.  Increase speed and beat until smooth and thick.

Yield: about 2 1/2 cups (20 servings)
One serving: 2 Tbl.
Calories per serving: 30
Exchanges: 1/3 milk

# Nutrient Analysis of Recipes*

| | Amount | Calories | Protein (grams) | Carbo-hydrate (grams) | Fat (grams) | Cholesterol (mg.) | CSI** (Units) | Dietary Fiber (grams) | Calcium (mg.) | Iron (mg.) | Sodium (mg.) | Potas-sium (mg.) |
|---|---|---|---|---|---|---|---|---|---|---|---|---|
| **APPETIZERS & DRESSINGS** | | | | | | | | | | | | |
| Creamy Seafood Dip | 2 Tbl. | 30 | 3.75 | 1.30 | 1.10 | 6 | 0.91 | 0.0 | 23 | 0.94 | 109 | 50 |
| Low Fat Ranch Dressing(package) | 1 Tbl. | 14 | 0.51 | 1.00 | 0.90 | 2 | 0.32 | 0.0 | 16 | 0.00 | 75 | 21 |
| Low Fat Ranch Dressing(spices) | 1 Tbl. | 14 | 0.51 | 1.00 | 0.90 | 2 | 0.32 | 0.0 | 16 | 0.00 | 28 | 21 |
| Mock Sour Cream | 2 Tbl. | 16 | 2.55 | 0.70 | 0.20 | 1 | 0.17 | 0.0 | 18 | 0.03 | 81 | 24 |
| Salt Free Swt. Rice Vinegar(Equal) | 1 Tbl. | 3 | 0.20 | 0.90 | 0.00 | 0 | 0.00 | 0.0 | 1 | 0.10 | 0 | 15 |
| Salt Free Swt. Rice Vinegar(sugar) | 1 Tbl. | 10 | 0.00 | 2.90 | 0.00 | 0 | 0.00 | 0.0 | 1 | 0.10 | 0 | 15 |
| Smoked Salmon Spread | 2 Tbl. | 64 | 4.66 | 1.20 | 4.60 | 20 | 3.13 | 0.0 | 47 | 0.07 | 157 | 93 |
| Spinach Dip | 1/4 cup | 41 | 2.25 | 4.90 | 1.50 | 4 | 0.50 | 0.4 | 79 | 0.34 | 93 | 131 |
| Tangy Tomato Dressing | 1 Tbl. | 6 | 0.18 | 1.40 | 0.00 | 0 | 0.00 | 0.2 | 3 | 0.16 | 10 | 50 |
| **BEVERAGES** | | | | | | | | | | | | |
| Banana Milk Shake (Equal) | 1 cup | 88 | 5.14 | 16.90 | 0.40 | 2 | 0.32 | 0.7 | 154 | 0.19 | 63 | 383 |
| Buttermilk Fruit Shake (Equal) | 1 cup | 89 | 5.16 | 15.90 | 1.20 | 4 | 0.91 | 1.4 | 147 | 0.16 | 128 | 356 |
| Fruit Milk Shake (Equal) | 1 cup | 85 | 5.28 | 16.30 | 0.30 | 2 | 0.25 | 1.4 | 156 | 0.15 | 63 | 374 |
| Juice Cooler | 1 1/2 cups | 59 | 0.84 | 13.40 | 0.10 | 0 | 0.00 | 0.2 | 11 | 0.12 | 39 | 237 |
| Orange Julius | 3/4 cup | 117 | 6.59 | 22.00 | 0.40 | 3 | 0.29 | 0.3 | 215 | 0.20 | 84 | 513 |
| Wake-Up Shake | 1 cup | 120 | 6.17 | 23.30 | 0.50 | 4 | 0.45 | 0.8 | 203 | 0.21 | 84 | 518 |
| Wine Cooler | 1 1/2 cups | 87 | 0.40 | 2.70 | 0.00 | 0 | 0.00 | 0.0 | 8 | 0.52 | 40 | 132 |
| Yogurt Fruit Shake (Equal) | 1 cup | 105 | 8.11 | 18.70 | 0.30 | 2 | 0.24 | 1.4 | 231 | 0.20 | 87 | 460 |
| **BREADS & BREADING** | | | | | | | | | | | | |
| Applesauce Oatmeal Coffee Cake | 1 piece | 168 | 3.82 | 29.60 | 4.30 | 0 | 0.41 | 1.2 | 36 | 1.32 | 95 | 139 |
| Blueberry Coffee Cake | 1 piece | 163 | 3.78 | 28.20 | 4.10 | 0 | 0.39 | 1.2 | 55 | 1.24 | 98 | 140 |

*Source: Computer analysis was done by Nutrition & Diet Services, 927 Rimrock Lane, Portland, Oregon 97222.  **Cholesterol-Saturated Fat Index    xx indicates data not available
Note: Ingredients listed as optional are not included in analysis.  If a choice of ingredients is given, the first one listed is used.

228

| | Amount | Calories | Protein (grams) | Carbo- hydrate (grams) | Fat (grams) | Cholesterol (mg.) | CSI** (Units) | Dietary Fiber (grams) | Calcium (mg.) | Iron (mg.) | Sodium (mg.) | Potas- sium (mg.) |
|---|---|---|---|---|---|---|---|---|---|---|---|---|
| Cottage Cheese Pancakes(Equal) | 2 | 122 | 10.14 | 18.20 | 0.60 | 2 | 0.37 | 0.6 | 48 | 1.58 | 196 | 113 |
| Cottage Cheese Pancakes(sugar) | 2 | 134 | 9.64 | 22.00 | 0.60 | 2 | 0.37 | 0.6 | 40 | 1.58 | 196 | 113 |
| Dumplings | 1 | 87 | 3.54 | 17.30 | 0.20 | 0 | 0.06 | 0.6 | 34 | 0.31 | 70 | 62 |
| Homemade Breading(salt-free bouillon) | 1 Tbl. | 26 | 0.56 | 6.20 | 0.00 | 0 | 0.00 | 0.3 | 0 | 0.50 | 141 | 12 |
| Homemade Breading(regular bouillon) | 1 Tbl. | 26 | 0.56 | 6.20 | 0.10 | 0 | 0.00 | 0.3 | 0 | 0.49 | 73 | 48 |
| Italian Focaccia Bread | 1/8 | 166 | 4.86 | 28.90 | 2.10 | 0 | 0.57 | 1.2 | 65 | 1.83 | 327 | 61 |
| Oat Bran Muffins | 1 | 113 | 4.36 | 23.50 | 3.50 | 0 | 0.46 | 3.5 | 55 | 1.39 | 94 | 230 |
| Refrigerator Bran Muffins | 1 | 138 | 3.56 | 24.60 | 4.70 | 1 | 0.43 | 3.4 | 31 | 2.03 | 181 | 164 |

## GRAVIES, SAUCES, AND TOPPINGS

| | Amount | Calories | Protein (grams) | Carbo- hydrate (grams) | Fat (grams) | Cholesterol (mg.) | CSI** (Units) | Dietary Fiber (grams) | Calcium (mg.) | Iron (mg.) | Sodium (mg.) | Potas- sium (mg.) |
|---|---|---|---|---|---|---|---|---|---|---|---|---|
| Cornstarch Gravy(salt-free broth) | 2 Tbl. | 6 | 0.28 | 1.30 | 0.00 | 0 | 0.00 | 0.0 | 0 | 0.01 | 11 | 78 |
| Cornstarch Gravy(regular broth) | 2 Tbl. | 6 | 0.28 | 1.30 | 0.00 | 0 | 0.00 | 0.0 | 0 | 0.01 | 126 | 2 |
| Flour Gravy(salt-free broth) | 2 Tbl. | 11 | 0.54 | 2.20 | 0.00 | 0 | 0.00 | 0.1 | 0 | 0.12 | 11 | 78 |
| Flour Gravy(regular broth) | 2 Tbl. | 11 | 0.54 | 2.20 | 0.00 | 0 | 0.00 | 0.1 | 0 | 0.12 | 126 | 5 |
| Fresh Cucumber Sauce | 1/4 cup | 42 | 1.07 | 2.60 | 2.90 | 6 | 0.89 | 0.2 | 38 | 0.15 | 96 | 75 |
| Spanish Yogurt Sauce | 1/4 cup | 39 | 2.87 | 7.00 | 0.90 | 0 | 0.08 | 0.0 | 83 | 0.53 | 230 | 100 |
| Thick and Chunky Salsa | 1/4 cup | 23 | 1.11 | 5.10 | 0.20 | 0 | 0.03 | 0.7 | 32 | 0.73 | 13 | 233 |

## BOTTTLED TOPPINGS:

| | Amount | Calories | Protein (grams) | Carbo- hydrate (grams) | Fat (grams) | Cholesterol (mg.) | CSI** (Units) | Dietary Fiber (grams) | Calcium (mg.) | Iron (mg.) | Sodium (mg.) | Potas- sium (mg.) |
|---|---|---|---|---|---|---|---|---|---|---|---|---|
| Kraft Sauceworks Sweet'n Sour Sauce | 1 Tbl. | 25 | 0.00 | 5.00 | 0.00 | 0 | 0.00 | xx | 0 | 0 | 50 | 8 |
| Lea & Perrins White Wine Worcestershire Sauce | 1 Tbl. | 9 | 1.00 | 1.00 | 1.00 | xx | xx | xx | xx | xx | 126 | xx |
| Lime Juice | 1 Tbl. | 4 | 0.00 | 1.00 | 0.00 | 0 | 0.00 | 0 | 1 | 0 | 0 | 17 |
| Milani 1890 Dill Sauce | 1 Tbl. | 1 | 0.00 | 0.00 | 0.00 | xx | 0.00 | xx | xx | xx | xx | xx |
| Old Spice Honey Mustard | 1 Tbl. | 37 | 0.75 | 7.10 | 1.00 | 0 | 0.12 | 0.17 | 7 | 0.28 | 88 | 19 |

**Cholesterol-Saturated Fat Index    xx indicates data not available
Note: Ingredients listed as optional are not included in analysis. If a choice of ingredients is given, the first one listed is used.

| | Amount | Calories | Protein (grams) | Carbohydrate (grams) | Fat (grams) | Cholesterol (mg.) | CSI** (Units) | Dietary Fiber (grams) | Calcium (mg.) | Iron (mg.) | Sodium (mg.) | Potassium (mg.) |
|---|---|---|---|---|---|---|---|---|---|---|---|---|
| Ragu 100% Natural Pizza Sauce | 1 Tbl. | 8 | 0.00 | 1.00 | 0.00 | 0 | 0.46 | 0 | 4 | 0 | 62 | 39 |
| S &W Mesquite Cooking Sauce & Marinade | 1 Tbl. | xx | xx | xx | xx | xx | xx | xx | xx | xx | xx | xx |
| Mustard Sauce(from dry) | 1 tsp. | 9 | 0.50 | 0.30 | 0.60 | 0 | 0.00 | 0.03 | 4 | 0.10 | 0 | 10 |

## SOUPS AND STEWS

| | Amount | Calories | Protein (grams) | Carbohydrate (grams) | Fat (grams) | Cholesterol (mg.) | CSI** (Units) | Dietary Fiber (grams) | Calcium (mg.) | Iron (mg.) | Sodium (mg.) | Potassium (mg.) |
|---|---|---|---|---|---|---|---|---|---|---|---|---|
| Chili Con Carne-turkey | 1 cup | 229 | 19.05 | 20.70 | 8.40 | 38 | 4.07 | 4.5 | 70 | 3.07 | 326 | 745 |
| Chili Con Carne-beef | 1 cup | 248 | 20.04 | 20.70 | 10.10 | 48 | 6.14 | 4.5 | 60 | 3.34 | 320 | 774 |
| Chilled Tomato Shrimp Soup | 1 1/4 cups | 108 | 15.25 | 11.50 | 0.80 | 124 | 6.42 | 1.0 | 48 | 3.43 | 173 | 671 |
| Clam Chowder (salt-free mix) | 1 cup | 166 | 14.55 | 23.60 | 1.10 | 21 | 1.28 | 0.7 | 256 | 7.96 | 207 | 947 |
| Clam Chowder (regular mix) | 1 cup | 166 | 14.55 | 23.60 | 1.10 | 21 | 1.28 | 0.7 | 256 | 7.96 | 776 | 662 |
| Cream of Mushroom Soup (salt-free mix) | 1 cup | 95 | 7.16 | 15.20 | 0.70 | 3 | 0.32 | 0.3 | 229 | 0.35 | 107 | 709 |
| Cream of Mushroom Soup (regular mix) | 1 cup | 95 | 7.16 | 15.20 | 0.70 | 3 | 0.32 | 0.3 | 229 | 0.35 | 678 | 424 |
| Cream of Vegetable Soup (salt-free mix) | 1 cup | 97 | 7.61 | 15.40 | 0.70 | 3 | 0.32 | 0.8 | 241 | 0.36 | 112 | 726 |
| Cream of Vegetable Soup (regular mix) | 1 cup | 97 | 7.61 | 15.40 | 0.70 | 3 | 0.32 | 0.8 | 241 | 0.36 | 683 | 441 |
| Cream Soup Mix (salt-free bouillon) | 1/3 cup, dry | 186 | 12.07 | 30.90 | 1.50 | 6 | 0.45 | 0.1 | 387 | 0.46 | 180 | 1501 |
| Cream Soup Mix (regular bouillon) | 1/3 cup, dry | 186 | 12.07 | 30.90 | 1.50 | 6 | 0.45 | 0.1 | 387 | 0.46 | 1890 | 592 |
| Fish Stew | 1 1/2 cups | 169 | 25.36 | 12.30 | 1.90 | 42 | 2.50 | 3.1 | 94 | 1.17 | 473 | 766 |
| French Onion Soup (salt-free broth) | 1/6 recipe | 135 | 8.98 | 16.50 | 3.50 | 8 | 2.24 | 1.2 | 140 | 0.92 | 225 | 724 |
| French Onion Soup (regular broth) | 1/6 recipe | 135 | 8.98 | 16.50 | 3.50 | 8 | 2.24 | 1.2 | 140 | 0.92 | 1038 | 100 |
| Italian Cioppino | 1 1/2 cups | 213 | 26.78 | 18.50 | 2.20 | 42 | 2.55 | 2.8 | 134 | 3.02 | 116 | 1287 |
| Minestrone Soup (salt-free broth) | 1 cup | 118 | 7.94 | 21.30 | 1.00 | 1 | 0.45 | 5.0 | 71 | 2.29 | 83 | 628 |
| Minestrone Soup (regular broth) | 1 cup | 118 | 7.94 | 21.30 | 1.00 | 1 | 0.45 | 5.0 | 71 | 2.29 | 344 | 420 |
| New England Clam Chowder | 1 cup | 151 | 18.43 | 16.00 | 1.00 | 28 | 1.71 | 0.9 | 131 | 0.40 | 111 | 595 |

**Cholesterol-Saturated Fat Index    xx indicates data not available

Note: Ingredients listed as optional are not included in analysis. If a choice of ingredients is given, the first one listed is used.

| | Amount | Calories | Protein (grams) | Carbo-hydrate (grams) | Fat (grams) | Cholesterol (mg.) | CSI** (Units) | Dietary Fiber (grams) | Calcium (mg.) | Iron (mg.) | Sodium (mg.) | Potassium (mg.) |
|---|---|---|---|---|---|---|---|---|---|---|---|---|
| Oriental Noodle Soup | 1 cup | 79 | 4.55 | 14.70 | 0.30 | 0 | 0.04 | 1.1 | 15 | 0.72 | 644 | 110 |
| Oriental Noodle Soup(salt-free broth) | 1 cup | 79 | 4.55 | 14.70 | 0.30 | 0 | 0.04 | 1.1 | 15 | 0.72 | 24 | 734 |
| Taco Soup-turkey | 1 cup | 149 | 11.50 | 14.90 | 4.90 | 23 | 2.48 | 3.7 | 66 | 2.08 | 210 | 555 |
| Taco Soup-beef | 1 cup | 161 | 12.17 | 14.90 | 6.00 | 28 | 3.72 | 3.7 | 60 | 2.24 | 207 | 572 |
| Three Bean Soup | 1 cup | 126 | 5.88 | 25.60 | 1.20 | 0 | 0.17 | 3.7 | 51 | 2.21 | 482 | 584 |
| Zero Vegetable Soup | 1 1/4 cups | 46 | 2.68 | 8.70 | 0.20 | 0 | 0.02 | 2.1 | 29 | 0.44 | 484 | 238 |
| Zero Vegetable Soup(salt-free broth) | 1 1/4 cups | 46 | 2.68 | 8.70 | 0.20 | 0 | 0.02 | 2.1 | 29 | 0.44 | 32 | 770 |
| **VEGETABLES** | | | | | | | | | | | | |
| Basil Tomatoes | 1/4 recipe | 18 | 0.70 | 3.80 | 0.20 | 0 | 0.03 | 1.1 | 12 | 0.49 | 7 | 178 |
| Gourmet Cucumbers | 1/4 recipe | 26 | 0.53 | 6.00 | 0.10 | 0 | 0.03 | 1.0 | 25 | 0.49 | 176 | 146 |
| Italian Herb Tomatoes | 1/4 recipe | 21 | 0.77 | 5.10 | 0.70 | 0 | 0.04 | 1.2 | 7 | 0.56 | 8 | 216 |
| Marinated Vegetables | 1/2 cup | 25 | 1.00 | 3.90 | 0.80 | 0.5 | 0.50 | 1.5 | 21 | 0.50 | 85 | 139 |
| Mexican Vegetables | 1/2 cup | 33 | 1.31 | 8.10 | 0.10 | 0 | 0.02 | 1.3 | 19 | 0.56 | 7 | 175 |
| Ranch Beans | 1/2 cup | 150 | 7.48 | 31.10 | 0.80 | 0 | 0.12 | 8.4 | 66 | 1.19 | 594 | 451 |
| Refried Beans | 1/4 recipe | 65 | 3.35 | 12.80 | 0.30 | 0 | 0.04 | 3.6 | 33 | 1.35 | 282 | 178 |
| Seasoned Green Beans | 1/4 recipe | 31 | 1.50 | 6.60 | 0.30 | 0 | 0.01 | 1.3 | 33 | 0.42 | 118 | 116 |
| Zucchini, Tomato, and Onion | 1/2 cup | 36 | 1.45 | 7.50 | 0.40 | 0 | 0.05 | 1.9 | 22 | 0.59 | 6 | 285 |
| **SALADS** | | | | | | | | | | | | |
| Apple Salad Mold | 1/2 cup | 35 | 1.03 | 7.50 | 0.10 | 0 | 0.02 | 0.8 | 10 | 0.17 | 52 | 95 |
| Broccoli Salad | 1 cup | 70 | 3.03 | 7.20 | 4.00 | 7 | 1.06 | 2.3 | 31 | 1.06 | 132 | 357 |
| Cabbage Salad | 1 cup | 54 | 1.86 | 8.00 | 2.30 | 0 | 0.33 | 1.9 | 84 | 1.20 | 191 | 255 |
| Chicken and Fruit Salad | 1 1/2 cups | 198 | 18.35 | 24.00 | 3.80 | 45 | 3.25 | 3.0 | 79 | 1.19 | 82 | 530 |

**Cholesterol-Saturated Fat Index   xx indicates data not available
Note: Ingredients listed as optional are not included in analysis. If a choice of ingredients is given, the first one listed is used.

| | Amount | Calories | Protein (grams) | Carbohydrate (grams) | Fat (grams) | Cholesterol (mg.) | CSI** (Units) | Dietary Fiber (grams) | Calcium (mg.) | Iron (mg.) | Sodium (mg.) | Potassium (mg.) |
|---|---|---|---|---|---|---|---|---|---|---|---|---|
| Chicken and Spinach Salad | 2 cups | 130 | 13.09 | 9.50 | 4.70 | 31 | 2.22 | 2.6 | 52 | 1.30 | 46 | 367 |
| Cinnamon Chicken Salad | 1 cup | 176 | 21.25 | 9.50 | 5.60 | 58 | 4.32 | 0.7 | 51 | 1.23 | 126 | 314 |
| Curry Tuna Salad | 3/4 cup | 181 | 24.99 | 6.60 | 5.50 | 37 | 3.01 | 0.3 | 16 | 3.15 | 592 | 324 |
| Fiesta Vegetable Salad | 1/2 cup | 80 | 2.31 | 6.10 | 5.10 | 11 | 1.45 | 1.0 | 53 | 0.28 | 184 | 178 |
| Fruit Salad | 1/2 cup | 54 | 1.83 | 11.90 | 0.40 | 1 | 0.12 | 1.3 | 49 | 0.19 | 21 | 270 |
| Greek Salad | 1 cup | 53 | 2.43 | 4.20 | 3.20 | 13 | 2.70 | 0.9 | 83 | 0.46 | 159 | 127 |
| Herb Potato Salad | 1/6 recipe | 81 | 1.90 | 16.20 | 1.10 | 2 | 0.28 | 0.2 | 19 | 0.27 | 60 | 308 |
| Lentil Rice Salad | 1 cup | 116 | 5.43 | 23.00 | 0.70 | 0 | 0.11 | 3.5 | 24 | 1.86 | 192 | 326 |
| Macaroni Salad | 1 cup | 174 | 3.91 | 26.30 | 5.80 | 10 | 1.59 | 2.0 | 22 | 1.28 | 433 | 155 |
| Oriental Rice & Seafood Salad | 1 cup | 140 | 14.46 | 18.20 | 1.00 | 111 | 5.82 | 1.4 | 38 | 2.51 | 573 | 230 |
| Seafood Salad | 1/2 cup | 89 | 8.43 | 7.40 | 2.60 | 17 | 1.63 | 0.3 | 50 | 0.32 | 553 | 127 |
| Shrimp Coleslaw | 1 cup | 75 | 9.29 | 8.30 | 0.50 | 64 | 3.32 | 1.5 | 104 | 1.60 | 224 | 318 |
| Three Bean Salad | 1/2 cup | 94 | 5.05 | 17.50 | 0.70 | 0 | 0.09 | 3.6 | 42 | 1.56 | 313 | 242 |
| Vegetable Bean Salad | 1/2 cup | 59 | 3.18 | 11.90 | 0.10 | 0 | 0.03 | 2.8 | 34 | 0.92 | 277 | 246 |

## RICE, POTATOES AND PASTA

| | Amount | Calories | Protein (grams) | Carbohydrate (grams) | Fat (grams) | Cholesterol (mg.) | CSI** (Units) | Dietary Fiber (grams) | Calcium (mg.) | Iron (mg.) | Sodium (mg.) | Potassium (mg.) |
|---|---|---|---|---|---|---|---|---|---|---|---|---|
| Herb and Vegetable Rice Blend(salt-free broth) | 3/4 cup | 118 | 3.26 | 24.20 | 1.20 | 0 | 0.22 | 2.2 | 23 | 0.66 | 33 | 464 |
| Herb and Vegetable Rice Blend(regular broth) | 3/4 cup | 118 | 3.26 | 24.20 | 1.20 | 0 | 0.22 | 2.2 | 23 | 0.66 | 459 | 158 |
| Herb Rice Blend(salt-free broth) | 1/2 cup | 112 | 2.86 | 22.90 | 1.00 | 0 | 0.21 | 1.7 | 14 | 0.43 | 13 | 362 |
| Herb Rice Blend(regular broth) | 1/2 cup | 112 | 2.86 | 22.90 | 1.00 | 0 | 0.21 | 1.7 | 14 | 0.43 | 439 | 56 |
| Low Fat French Fries | 1/4 recipe | 183 | 3.21 | 35.20 | 3.60 | 0 | 0.28 | 1.6 | 14 | 1.90 | 11 | 582 |
| Microwave Baked Potatoes | 1 medium | 152 | 3.21 | 35.20 | 0.10 | 0 | 0.28 | 1.6 | 14 | 1.90 | 11 | 582 |

**Cholesterol-Saturated Fat Index    xx indicates data not available
Note: Ingredients listed as optional are not included in analysis. If a choice of ingredients is given, the first one listed is used.

| | Amount | Calories | Protein (grams) | Carbo-hydrate (grams) | Fat (grams) | Cholesterol (mg.) | CSI** (Units) | Dietary Fiber (grams) | Calcium (mg.) | Iron (mg.) | Sodium (mg.) | Potas-sium (mg.) |
|---|---|---|---|---|---|---|---|---|---|---|---|---|
| Scalloped Potatoes | 1/6 recipe | 114 | 4.12 | 24.20 | 0.20 | 1 | 0.14 | 0.4 | 83 | 0.47 | 64 | 463 |
| Tomato and Basil Pasta | 1 cup | 169 | 5.84 | 34.40 | 1.00 | 0 | 0.14 | 3.0 | 20 | 2.03 | 9 | 246 |
| **SANDWICHES** | | | | | | | | | | | | |
| Fruit and Ricotta Sandwich | 1 | 156 | 9.01 | 24.60 | 3.20 | 8 | 1.77 | 3.6 | 105 | 1.29 | 413 | 289 |
| Meatball Sandwich-turkey | 1 | 303 | 17.61 | 39.90 | 7.40 | 28 | 3.56 | 1.4 | 53 | 2.94 | 300 | 432 |
| Meatball Sandwich-beef | 1 | 317 | 18.34 | 39.90 | 8.60 | 35 | 5.08 | 1.4 | 46 | 3.14 | 295 | 454 |
| Tomato and Ricotta Sandwich | 1 | 130 | 8.91 | 17.00 | 3.50 | 8 | 1.78 | 2.6 | 101 | 1.33 | 485 | 213 |
| Turkey French Dip | one serving | 355 | 22.79 | 48.20 | 6.80 | 36 | 5.51 | 1.5 | 227 | 2.91 | 592 | 364 |
| **PIZZA** | | | | | | | | | | | | |
| Boboli Pizza-Sausage Style | 2 slices | 218 | 12.75 | 26.50 | 7.20 | 19 | 3.30 | 1.1 | 173 | 2.23 | 573 | 146 |
| Boboli Pizza-Shrimp Style | 2 slices | 241 | 17.38 | 29.10 | 6.30 | 74 | 5.79 | 1.2 | 182 | 2.90 | 617 | 201 |
| Crusty Calzone-Turkey Sausage | 1 slice | 231 | 12.90 | 30.00 | 6.50 | 25 | 3.62 | 0.6 | 121 | 1.83 | 608 | 205 |
| Crusty Calzone-Ground Beef | 1 slice | 243 | 14.28 | 28.60 | 8.00 | 28 | 5.02 | 2.4 | 143 | 1.75 | 374 | 166 |
| Crusty Calzone-Ground Turkey | 1 slice | 236 | 13.91 | 28.60 | 7.30 | 24 | 4.26 | 2.4 | 147 | 1.65 | 376 | 155 |
| Crusty Calzone-Turkey Ham | 1 slice | 225 | 14.11 | 28.90 | 5.90 | 46 | 4.48 | 0.3 | 120 | 2.02 | 640 | 210 |
| Crusty Calzone-Sliced Turkey | 1 slice | 229 | 17.16 | 27.80 | 5.40 | 29 | 3.44 | 0.3 | 121 | 1.62 | 377 | 205 |
| Focaccia Pizza | 1 slice | 207 | 9.03 | 30.20 | 4.30 | 8 | 2.46 | 1.3 | 169 | 1.87 | 463 | 110 |
| Individual Pizza | 1 | 179 | 8.52 | 27.20 | 3.80 | 9 | 2.25 | 1.5 | 123 | 1.46 | 319 | 298 |
| **STUFFED POTATOES** | | | | | | | | | | | | |
| Cheese Stuffed Potatoes | 1/2 potato | 99 | 5.24 | 18.80 | 0.40 | 1 | 0.26 | 0.8 | 28 | 1.02 | 122 | 327 |
| Cheese & Chicken-Potato Topping | 1/4 recipe | 261 | 18.04 | 41.30 | 3.00 | 33 | 2.98 | 2.3 | 135 | 2.60 | 392 | 824 |

**Cholesterol-Saturated Fat Index    xx indicates data not available
Note: Ingredients listed as optional are not included in analysis. If a choice of ingredients is given, the first one listed is used.

| | Amount | Calories | Protein (grams) | Carbohydrate (grams) | Fat (grams) | Cholesterol (mg.) | CSI** (Units) | Dietary Fiber (grams) | Calcium (mg.) | Iron (mg.) | Sodium (mg.) | Potassium (mg.) |
|---|---|---|---|---|---|---|---|---|---|---|---|---|
| Ground Beef and Mushroom-Potato Topping | 1/4 recipe | 304 | 16.39 | 44.00 | 7.30 | 35 | 4.64 | 2.9 | 53 | 3.82 | 61 | 1048 |
| Ground Turkey and Mushroom-Potato Topping | 1/4 recipe | 290 | 15.66 | 44.00 | 6.10 | 28 | 3.10 | 2.9 | 60 | 3.62 | 66 | 1026 |
| Pizza-Potato Topping-turkey | 1/4 recipe | 298 | 16.19 | 42.70 | 7.30 | 33 | 4.14 | 2.9 | 100 | 3.14 | 189 | 890 |
| Pizza-Potato Topping-beef | 1/4 recipe | 312 | 16.92 | 42.70 | 8.50 | 40 | 5.68 | 2.9 | 93 | 3.34 | 184 | 912 |
| **MEATLESS ENTREES** | | | | | | | | | | | | |
| Egg Foo Yung(salt-free broth) | 1/4 recipe | 61 | 6.66 | 8.10 | 0.10 | 53 | 0.03 | 0.9 | 25 | 1.29 | 174 | 337 |
| Egg Foo Yung(regular broth) | 1/4 recipe | 61 | 6.66 | 8.10 | 0.10 | 53 | 0.03 | 0.9 | 25 | 1.29 | 362 | 188 |
| Fruit and Ricotta Split | 1 recipe | 184 | 12.92 | 23.90 | 4.50 | 16 | 3.36 | 2.6 | 173 | 0.97 | 521 | 459 |
| Italian Broccoli and Pasta | 1/4 recipe | 151 | 7.49 | 29.70 | 1.30 | 1 | 0.34 | 5.2 | 94 | 2.73 | 54 | 541 |
| Italian Zucchini Frittata | 1/4 recipe | 67 | 8.36 | 7.20 | 1.00 | 2 | 0.64 | 2.1 | 97 | 2.03 | 134 | 538 |
| Puffy Chile Relleno Casserole | 1/8 recipe | 295 | 26.42 | 22.10 | 11.10 | 30 | 7.92 | 1.4 | 495 | 2.89 | 471 | 263 |
| Quick Lasagna | 1/12 recipe | 242 | 15.29 | 32.00 | 5.87 | 13 | 3.61 | 1.13 | 178 | 1.52 | 609 | 261 |
| Spanish Zucchini Frittata | 1/4 omelet | 61 | 7.50 | 8.10 | 0.20 | 0 | 0.06 | 2.4 | 62 | 2.14 | 91 | 536 |
| Vegetables Primavera | 1/5 recipe | 220 | 7.90 | 40.60 | 3.10 | 0 | 1.04 | 4.3 | 61 | 1.86 | 499 | 493 |
| **POULTRY** | | | | | | | | | | | | |
| Baked Chicken (only) with Bottled Topping, page 229 | 1/4 recipe | 151 | 28.28 | 0.00 | 3.30 | 77 | 4.79 | 0.0 | 14 | 0.94 | 67 | 233 |
| Baked Chimichangas | 1/4 recipe | 275 | 21.92 | 32.00 | 6.90 | 46 | 4.73 | 1.3 | 155 | 2.12 | 445 | 238 |
| Chicken á la Soda | 1/6 recipe | 158 | 27.31 | 3.50 | 3.20 | 73 | 4.54 | 0.8 | 22 | 1.13 | 129 | 323 |
| Chicken and Pea Pod Stir-Fry | 1/5 recipe | 190 | 25.83 | 12.60 | 2.30 | 62 | 3.89 | 2.6 | 63 | 2.58 | 388 | 486 |

**Cholesterol-Saturated Fat Index    xx indicates data not available

Note: Ingredients listed as optional are not included in analysis. If a choice of ingredients is given, the first one listed is used.

| | Amount | Calories | Protein (grams) | Carbo-hydrate (grams) | Fat (grams) | Cholesterol (mg.) | CSI** (Units) | Dietary Fiber (grams) | Calcium (mg.) | Iron (mg.) | Sodium (mg.) | Potas-sium (mg.) |
|---|---|---|---|---|---|---|---|---|---|---|---|---|
| Chicken Breasts Florentine | 1/6 recipe | 213 | 33.63 | 9.00 | 4.50 | 80 | 5.63 | 2.1 | 222 | 2.56 | 219 | 547 |
| Chicken Breasts in Mushroom Sauce | 1/4 recipe | 206 | 32.60 | 8.20 | 3.50 | 78 | 4.83 | 0.7 | 82 | 1.76 | 373 | 473 |
| Chicken Breasts Supreme | 1/8 recipe | 190 | 29.46 | 8.00 | 3.50 | 77 | 4.81 | 0.7 | 18 | 1.67 | 252 | 330 |
| Chicken Cacciatore | 1/6 recipe | 232 | 32.53 | 15.70 | 3.80 | 77 | 4.79 | 2.4 | 61 | 2.66 | 130 | 676 |
| Chicken Enchiladas | 1/8 recipe | 276 | 22.21 | 30.40 | 7.10 | 42 | 6.09 | 2.0 | 284 | 2.20 | 653 | 516 |
| Chicken Fajitas | 1/4 recipe | 321 | 32.83 | 32.10 | 6.20 | 77 | 5.12 | 2.3 | 61 | 2.31 | 151 | 416 |
| Chicken in Gravy(salt-free broth) | 1/6 recipe | 190 | 30.10 | 7.90 | 3.40 | 77 | 4.79 | 1.5 | 26 | 1.59 | 100 | 504 |
| Chicken in Gravy(regular broth) | 1/6 recipe | 190 | 30.10 | 7.90 | 3.40 | 77 | 4.79 | 1.5 | 26 | 1.59 | 303 | 372 |
| Chicken in Salsa | 1/4 recipe | 170 | 29.03 | 5.00 | 3.40 | 77 | 4.79 | 0.1 | 29 | 1.47 | 295 | 248 |
| Chicken Nuggets | 1/4 recipe | 203 | 29.42 | 12.30 | 3.30 | 77 | 4.81 | 0.5 | 16 | 1.97 | 350 | 260 |
| Chicken Picadillo | 1/4 recipe | 192 | 29.76 | 9.70 | 3.60 | 77 | 4.81 | 1.1 | 45 | 1.99 | 296 | 351 |
| Cooked and Cubed Chicken | 1/8 recipe | 111 | 20.21 | 0.00 | 2.80 | 53 | 3.46 | 0.0 | 9 | 0.66 | 45 | 126 |
| Crispy Potato Chicken | 1/4 recipe | 207 | 29.52 | 8.10 | 5.40 | 77 | 4.88 | 0.1 | 24 | 1.30 | 269 | 379 |
| French Glazed Chicken | 1/4 recipe | 189 | 28.39 | 7.60 | 4.20 | 78 | 4.94 | 0.1 | 20 | 1.10 | 206 | 278 |
| Mexican Chicken Casserole (salt-free soup mix) | 1/8 recipe | 321 | 31.02 | 31.20 | 7.50 | 64 | 6.05 | 1.4 | 256 | 1.91 | 267 | 638 |
| Mexican Chicken Casserole (regular soup mix) | 1/8 recipe | 321 | 31.02 | 31.20 | 7.50 | 64 | 6.05 | 1.4 | 256 | 1.91 | 677 | 428 |
| Mexican Style Chicken and Rice | 1/8 recipe | 285 | 32.38 | 25.80 | 5.60 | 78 | 5.79 | 2.5 | 93 | 1.74 | 274 | 448 |
| Oven Fried Chicken | 1/6 recipe | 168 | 28.62 | 4.10 | 3.30 | 77 | 4.79 | 0.2 | 13 | 1.25 | 139 | 239 |
| Polynesian Chicken(Sauce) | 1/8 recipe | 211 | 28.82 | 14.00 | 3.40 | 77 | 4.79 | 0.0 | 21 | 1.30 | 584 | 278 |
| Polynesian Chicken(Quick) | 1/8 recipe | 186 | 28.82 | 7.30 | 3.40 | 77 | 4.79 | 0.0 | 21 | 1.30 | 198 | 233 |
| Rolled Chicken and Asparagus | 1/4 recipe | 180 | 30.75 | 5.80 | 3.50 | 77 | 4.86 | 1.6 | 47 | 1.01 | 73 | 569 |
| Sausage and Sauerkraut | 1/5 recipe | 212 | 15.49 | 22.60 | 6.70 | 48 | 4.65 | 2.2 | 62 | 4.46 | 1206 | 729 |

**Cholesterol-Saturated Fat Index    xx indicates data not available
Note: Ingredients listed as optional are not included in analysis. If a choice of ingredients is given, the first one listed is used.

| | Amount | Calories | Protein (grams) | Carbo-hydrate (grams) | Fat (grams) | Cholesterol (mg.) | CSI** (Units) | Dietary Fiber (grams) | Calcium (mg.) | Iron (mg.) | Sodium (mg.) | Potassium (mg.) |
|---|---|---|---|---|---|---|---|---|---|---|---|---|
| Sweet and Sour Chicken | 1/5 recipe | 232 | 24.03 | 27.60 | 2.80 | 62 | 3.86 | 1.3 | 44 | 1.51 | 343 | 430 |
| Yogurt Cumin Chicken | 1/4 recipe | 181 | 29.41 | 6.30 | 3.40 | 77 | 4.83 | 0.1 | 56 | 1.31 | 99 | 308 |
| Stir-Fry | 1/4 recipe | 135 | 18.24 | 12.70 | 2.10 | 38 | 2.39 | 3.7 | 74 | 1.58 | 166 | 489 |
| **SEAFOOD** | | | | | | | | | | | | |
| Baked Fish (only) with Bottled Topping, page 229 | 1/4 recipe | 108 | 22.35 | 0.00 | 1.50 | 40 | 2.31 | 0.0 | 34 | 0.20 | 48 | 443 |
| Clam Fettucini | 1 cup | 225 | 15.00 | 36.50 | 1.50 | 24 | 1.36 | 1.9 | 46 | 11.68 | 138 | 272 |
| Crab Delight | 1/4 recipe | 98 | 8.59 | 15.00 | 0.70 | 11 | 0.55 | 0.6 | 33 | 1.13 | 502 | 207 |
| Fillets of Sole Thermidor | 1/8 recipe | 153 | 25.15 | 3.80 | 2.80 | 45 | 3.44 | 0.0 | 111 | 0.26 | 133 | 508 |
| Fish in Salsa | 1/4 recipe | 127 | 23.10 | 5.00 | 1.60 | 40 | 2.31 | 0.1 | 49 | 0.73 | 276 | 458 |
| French Glazed Fish | 1/4 recipe | 146 | 22.46 | 7.60 | 2.40 | 41 | 2.46 | 0.1 | 40 | 0.32 | 187 | 488 |
| Lemon Fish | 1/4 recipe | 121 | 22.44 | 0.70 | 1.50 | 40 | 2.31 | 0.0 | 37 | 0.34 | 71 | 469 |
| Oven Fried Fish (salt-free breading) | 1/4 recipe | 134 | 22.91 | 6.20 | 1.60 | 40 | 2.31 | 0.3 | 34 | 0.69 | 121 | 491 |
| Oven Fried Fish (regular breading) | 1/4 recipe | 134 | 22.91 | 6.20 | 1.60 | 40 | 2.31 | 0.3 | 34 | 0.69 | 189 | 455 |
| Oven Fried Oysters (salt-free breading) | 1/4 recipe | 124 | 8.39 | 16.40 | 2.60 | 56 | 3.46 | 0.5 | 48 | 7.89 | 261 | 334 |
| Oven Fried Oysters (regular breading) | 1/4 recipe | 124 | 8.39 | 16.40 | 2.60 | 56 | 3.46 | 0.5 | 48 | 7.89 | 398 | 261 |
| Poached Fish | 1/4 recipe | 108 | 22.39 | 0.00 | 1.50 | 40 | 2.31 | 0.0 | 34 | 0.20 | 120 | 444 |
| Salmon Cakes | 1 cake | 247 | 21.69 | 5.40 | 14.20 | 73 | 6.48 | 0.3 | 163 | 0.48 | 628 | 419 |
| Seafood Marinade-Soy | 1/2 Tbl. | 23 | 0.13 | 0.20 | 2.20 | 0 | 0.16 | 0.0 | 0 | 0.06 | 135 | 6 |
| Seafood Marinade-Lemon Basil | 1/2 Tbl. | 16 | 0.02 | 0.40 | 1.80 | 0 | 0.23 | 0.0 | 0 | 0.02 | 0 | 7 |
| Spanish Baked Fish | 1/4 recipe | 140 | 24.38 | 6.30 | 1.60 | 42 | 2.45 | 1.3 | 52 | 0.86 | 89 | 740 |
| Stir-Fry | 1/4 recipe | 102 | 12.98 | 12.80 | 0.90 | 83 | 4.32 | 3.7 | 83 | 2.42 | 228 | 450 |
| Sweet Mustard Fish | 1/4 recipe | 166 | 23.40 | 12.40 | 2.60 | 40 | 2.31 | 0.1 | 51 | 0.75 | 401 | 468 |

**Cholesterol-Saturated Fat Index    xx indicates data not available

Note: Ingredients listed as optional are not included in analysis. If a choice of ingredients is given, the first one listed is used.

| | Amount | Calories | Protein (grams) | Carbo-hydrate (grams) | Fat (grams) | Cholesterol (mg.) | CSI** (Units) | Dietary Fiber (grams) | Calcium (mg.) | Iron (mg.) | Sodium (mg.) | Potas-sium (mg.) |
|---|---|---|---|---|---|---|---|---|---|---|---|---|
| Tarragon Fish | 1/4 recipe | 146 | 26.08 | 2.70 | 2.80 | 45 | 3.33 | 0.0 | 149 | 0.38 | 109 | 537 |
| Yogurt Cumin Fish | 1/4 recipe | 138 | 23.48 | 6.30 | 1.60 | 40 | 2.35 | 0.1 | 76 | 0.59 | 80 | 518 |
| **BEEF AND PORK** | | | | | | | | | | | | |
| Beef Fajitas | 1/4 recipe | 342 | 30.02 | 31.50 | 10.50 | 75 | 6.62 | 2.3 | 54 | 4.28 | 139 | 510 |
| Chinese Barbecued Pork | 2 oz. | 106 | 16.67 | 2.70 | 2.80 | 53 | 3.59 | 0.0 | 5 | 0.88 | 129 | 306 |
| Chinese Pepper Steak | 1/5 recipe | 200 | 22.74 | 12.60 | 6.20 | 60 | 5.18 | 1.6 | 30 | 2.45 | 512 | 517 |
| Fajitas Barbecue Style | 1/4 recipe | 361 | 32.23 | 31.30 | 11.00 | 80 | 8.31 | 2.3 | 111 | 4.55 | 198 | 608 |
| Marinated Steak | 1/6 recipe | 191 | 26.56 | 2.80 | 7.30 | 75 | 6.41 | 0.1 | 17 | 2.76 | 609 | 430 |
| Orange Pork Chops | 1/4 recipe | 223 | 24.20 | 11.30 | 8.60 | 71 | 6.18 | 0.8 | 34 | 1.35 | 293 | 450 |
| Pork Chop Suey | 1/5 recipe | 163 | 20.80 | 11.50 | 3.30 | 61 | 4.00 | 1.4 | 41 | 1.50 | 460 | 569 |
| Pork Fajitas | 1/4 recipe | 308 | 29.04 | 31.50 | 6.90 | 79 | 5.50 | 2.2 | 52 | 2.68 | 141 | 630 |
| Stir-Fry: Beef | 1/4 recipe | 142 | 16.20 | 12.70 | 3.80 | 35 | 3.04 | 3.7 | 70 | 2.25 | 160 | 549 |
| Stir-Fry: Pork | 1/4 recipe | 158 | 15.46 | 12.70 | 5.90 | 39 | 3.91 | 3.7 | 70 | 1.63 | 162 | 526 |
| **GROUND MEAT DISHES** | | | | | | | | | | | | |
| Baked Meatballs-Beef | 3 meatballs | 137 | 12.78 | 4.40 | 7.20 | 35 | 4.61 | 0.1 | 29 | 1.41 | 47 | 189 |
| Baked Meatballs-Turkey | 3 meatballs | 123 | 12.05 | 4.40 | 6.00 | 28 | 3.07 | 0.1 | 36 | 1.21 | 52 | 167 |
| Bean and Beef Enchiladas | 1/12 recipe | 257 | 15.41 | 31.40 | 8.20 | 25 | 4.93 | 6.4 | 149 | 3.27 | 630 | 545 |
| Bean and Turkey Enchiladas | 1/12 recipe | 249 | 15.05 | 31.40 | 7.50 | 21 | 4.14 | 6.5 | 153 | 4.13 | 633 | 533 |
| Meat Patties-Beef | 1/6 recipe | 184 | 17.17 | 6.00 | 9.80 | 48 | 6.18 | 0.1 | 37 | 1.86 | 64 | 255 |
| Meat Patties-Turkey | 1/6 recipe | 165 | 16.18 | 6.00 | 8.10 | 38 | 4.11 | 0.1 | 47 | 1.59 | 70 | 226 |
| Ground Beef and Bean Casserole | 1/6 recipe | 233 | 18.73 | 19.60 | 9.70 | 48 | 6.16 | 6.8 | 50 | 1.64 | 432 | 471 |
| Ground Turkey and Bean Casserole | 1/6 recipe | 214 | 17.74 | 19.60 | 8.00 | 38 | 4.10 | 6.8 | 60 | 1.37 | 438 | 442 |

**Cholesterol-Saturated Fat Index    xx indicates data not available
Note: Ingredients listed as optional are not included in analysis. If a choice of ingredients is given, the first one listed is used.

| | Amount | Calories | Protein (grams) | Carbohydrate (grams) | Fat (grams) | Cholesterol (mg.) | CSI** (Units) | Dietary Fiber (grams) | Calcium (mg.) | Iron (mg.) | Sodium (mg.) | Potassium (mg.) |
|---|---|---|---|---|---|---|---|---|---|---|---|---|
| Ground Beef, Cabbage, and Noodle Cass.(reg.mix) | 1/7 recipe | 185 | 11.45 | 24.50 | 4.50 | 22 | 2.77 | 2.2 | 86 | 1.74 | 279 | 345 |
| Ground Beef, Cabbage, and Noodle Cass.(salt-free mix) | 1/7 recipe | 185 | 11.45 | 24.50 | 4.50 | 22 | 2.77 | 2.2 | 86 | 1.74 | 55 | 458 |
| Ground Turkey, Cabbage, and Noodle Cass.(reg. mix) | 1/7 recipe | 177 | 11.02 | 24.50 | 3.80 | 18 | 1.88 | 2.2 | 90 | 1.62 | 282 | 332 |
| Ground Turkey, Cabbage, and Noodle Cass.(salt-free mix) | 1/7 recipe | 177 | 11.02 | 24.50 | 3.80 | 18 | 1.88 | 2.2 | 90 | 1.62 | 56 | 445 |
| John Torrey-Beef | 1 cup | 220 | 13.48 | 28.10 | 6.20 | 27 | 3.98 | 2.5 | 106 | 2.40 | 145 | 462 |
| John Torrey-Turkey | 1 cup | 212 | 13.05 | 28.10 | 5.50 | 23 | 3.09 | 2.5 | 110 | 2.28 | 148 | 449 |
| Meat Loaf-Beef | 1/8 recipe | 228 | 19.34 | 12.20 | 11.10 | 53 | 6.92 | 0.8 | 50 | 2.23 | 253 | 408 |
| Meat Loaf-Turkey | 1/8 recipe | 206 | 18.24 | 12.20 | 9.20 | 43 | 4.62 | 0.8 | 62 | 1.92 | 260 | 375 |
| Moore-Beef | 1 cup | 330 | 23.20 | 28.10 | 13.50 | 61 | 8.36 | 1.3 | 66 | 3.45 | 514 | 368 |
| Moore-Turkey | 1 cup | 306 | 22.03 | 28.10 | 11.50 | 50 | 5.90 | 1.3 | 78 | 3.12 | 521 | 333 |
| Pizza Meat Loaf-Beef | 1/4 recipe | 250 | 24.03 | 2.40 | 15.40 | 75 | 10.07 | 0.4 | 64 | 2.13 | 160 | 336 |
| Pizza Meat Loaf-Turkey | 1/4 recipe | 221 | 22.56 | 2.40 | 12.90 | 61 | 6.99 | 0.4 | 79 | 1.72 | 169 | 292 |
| Sloppy Joes-Beef | 1/8 recipe | 253 | 15.16 | 25.30 | 9.70 | 36 | 5.20 | 1.6 | 69 | 2.54 | 620 | 223 |
| Sloppy Joes-Turkey | 1/8 recipe | 239 | 14.43 | 25.30 | 8.50 | 29 | 3.66 | 1.6 | 76 | 2.34 | 625 | 201 |
| Spaghetti and Meatballs-Beef | 1/6 recipe | 305 | 18.11 | 35.20 | 9.70 | 35 | 5.44 | 1.8 | 52 | 2.71 | 438 | 402 |
| Spaghetti and Meatballs-Turkey | 1/6 recipe | 291 | 17.38 | 35.20 | 8.50 | 28 | 3.89 | 1.8 | 59 | 2.51 | 443 | 380 |
| Swedish Meatballs-Beef-regular broth | 1/5 recipe | 206 | 8.41 | 10.30 | 10.10 | 48 | 6.18 | 0.2 | 37 | 2.08 | 364 | 257 |
| Swedish Meatballs-Beef-salt-free broth | 1/5 recipe | 206 | 8.41 | 10.30 | 10.10 | 48 | 6.18 | 0.2 | 37 | 2.08 | 68 | 499 |
| Swedish Meatballs-Turkey, 30% less salt broth | 1/5 recipe | 187 | 17.42 | 10.30 | 8.40 | 38 | 4.12 | 0.2 | 47 | 1.81 | 302 | 228 |

**Cholesterol-Saturated Fat Index    xx indicates data not available

Note: Ingredients listed as optional are not included in analysis. If a choice of ingredients is given, the first one listed is used.

| | Amount | Calories | Protein (grams) | Carbo-hydrate (grams) | Fat (grams) | Cholesterol (mg.) | CSI** (Units) | Dietary Fiber (grams) | Calcium (mg.) | Iron (mg.) | Sodium (mg.) | Potas-sium (mg.) |
|---|---|---|---|---|---|---|---|---|---|---|---|---|
| Swedish Meatballs-Turkey-salt-free broth | 1/5 recipe | 187 | 17.42 | 10.30 | 8.40 | 38 | 4.12 | 0.2 | 47 | 1.81 | 74 | 470 |
| Tortilla Pie-Beef | 1/12 recipe | 297 | 20.53 | 28.30 | 11.90 | 55 | 7.52 | 2.2 | 143 | 2.82 | 466 | 423 |
| Tortilla Pie-Turkey | 1/12 recipe | 278 | 19.54 | 28.30 | 10.20 | 45 | 4.54 | 2.2 | 153 | 2.55 | 472 | 394 |
| **DESSERTS** | | | | | | | | | | | | |
| Apple Cake | 1/16 recipe | 144 | 2.38 | 27.30 | 3.90 | 0 | 0.32 | 1.6 | 14 | 0.79 | 103 | 100 |
| Apple Crisp | 1/8 recipe | 80 | 0.90 | 16.00 | 2.00 | 0 | 0.35 | 1.1 | 10 | 0.40 | 22 | 98 |
| Baked Apple | 1/4 recipe | 65 | 0.23 | 16.90 | 0.40 | 0 | 0.06 | 2.4 | 10 | 0.25 | 4 | 128 |
| Butterfly Cup Cakes | 1 cupcake | 126 | 1.86 | 20.50 | 4.00 | 10 | 1.67 | 0.8 | 62 | 0.20 | 191 | 45 |
| Chocolate Cake | 1/16 recipe | 266 | 2.90 | 43.60 | 9.90 | 0 | 1.02 | 0.6 | 7 | 1.41 | 147 | 68 |
| Cream Cheese Dessert | 1/8 recipe | 202 | 7.76 | 26.90 | 7.70 | 24 | 5.85 | 0.0 | 176 | 0.31 | 554 | 231 |
| Fruit and Cake | 1 serving | 161 | 3.33 | 37.90 | 0.40 | 0 | 0.09 | 0.5 | 49 | 0.33 | 270 | 164 |
| Fruit Pizza for a Crowd | 1/18 recipe | 187 | 4.55 | 24.10 | 7.50 | 15 | 3.53 | 0.9 | 69 | 0.15 | 321 | 149 |
| Fruit Slush-Equal | 1 recipe | 80 | 5.35 | 14.10 | 0.60 | 2 | 0.26 | 2.9 | 167 | 0.48 | 64 | 388 |
| Fruit Slush-Sugar | 1 recipe | 92 | 4.85 | 17.90 | 0.60 | 2 | 0.26 | 2.9 | 167 | 0.48 | 64 | 388 |
| Mandarin Orange Cake | 1/9 recipe | 141 | 2.14 | 26.70 | 3.00 | 0 | 0.24 | 0.5 | 10 | 0.88 | 124 | 52 |
| Mock Plum Pudding | 1/9 recipe | 164 | 3.29 | 35.60 | 2.60 | 0 | 0.29 | 3.4 | 23 | 1.12 | 116 | 262 |
| Pineapple Cake | 1/16 recipe | 128 | 2.48 | 29.90 | 0.20 | 0 | 0.02 | 0.7 | 10 | 0.99 | 157 | 71 |
| Sauce Topped Cake | 1/7 recipe | 206 | 5.64 | 42.80 | 0.30 | 1 | 0.16 | 1.6 | 121 | 0.30 | 301 | 349 |
| **SWEET SAUCES, GLAZES AND TOPPINGS** | | | | | | | | | | | | |
| Chocolate Glaze | 2 tsp. | 27 | 0.22 | 6.70 | 0.10 | 0 | 0.04 | 0.0 | 6 | 0.04 | 3 | 13 |
| Cream Cheese Topping | 2 Tbl. | 31 | 1.75 | 2.80 | 1.50 | 4 | 1.18 | 0.0 | 42 | 0.01 | 118 | 56 |

**Cholesterol-Saturated Fat Index    xx indicates data not available
Note: Ingredients listed as optional are not included in analysis. If a choice of ingredients is given, the first one listed is used.

| | Amount | Calories | Protein (grams) | Carbo-hydrate (grams) | Fat (grams) | Cholesterol (mg.) | CSI** (Units) | Dietary Fiber (grams) | Calcium (mg.) | Iron (mg.) | Sodium (mg.) | Potas-sium (mg.) |
|---|---|---|---|---|---|---|---|---|---|---|---|---|
| Cream Glaze | 2 tsp. | 26 | 0.17 | 6.50 | 0.00 | 0 | 0.00 | 0.0 | 6 | 0.00 | 3 | 8 |
| Fruit Sauce-Equal | 1/4 cup | 15 | 0.58 | 3.30 | 0.20 | 0 | 0.01 | 1.2 | 6 | 0.17 | 1 | 78 |
| Fruit Sauce-Sugar | 1/4 cup | 26 | 0.28 | 6.50 | 0.20 | 0 | 0.01 | 1.2 | 6 | 0.17 | 1 | 78 |
| Liqueur Sauce | 1/4 cup | 81 | 2.08 | 11.40 | 0.10 | 1 | 0.06 | 0.1 | 67 | 0.12 | 26 | 155 |
| Orange Glaze | 2 tsp. | 26 | 0.03 | 6.80 | 0.00 | 0 | 0.00 | 0.0 | 0 | 0.00 | 0 | 9 |
| Pina Colada Sauce | 1/4 cup | 44 | 2.03 | 4.10 | 0.10 | 1 | 0.15 | 0.0 | 72 | 0.00 | 32 | 107 |

**Cholesterol-Saturated Fat Index    xx indicates data not available

Note: Ingredients listed as optional are not included in analysis. If a choice of ingredients is given, the first one listed is used.

# WEEKLY GROCERY LIST

**Milk/Yogurt/Cheese/Eggs**

_____

_____

_____

**Canned & Packaged Foods**

_____

_____

_____

**Breads & Cereals**

_____

_____

_____

**Frozen Foods**

_____

_____

_____

**Fresh Vegetables**
(choose for salad or raw and 2 for cooking)

_____

_____

_____

**Fresh Fruit** (2-3)

_____

_____

_____

**Meat/Poultry/Seafood**

_____

_____

_____

**Sandwich/Lunch Makings**

_____

_____

_____

**Miscellaneous**

_____

_____

_____

_____

_____

_____

Choose an entreé for each main meal and check ingredients needed and add them to this list.

# GROCERY LIST: STAPLES

**Spices and Baking Products**
allspice
dried basil
bay leaves
celery seed
chili powder
dried cilantro
cinnamon
ground cloves
coriander
cumin
curry
dried dill
garlic powder
ginger
Italian herb seasoning
Kitchen Bouquet
liquid smoke
dried marjoram
nutmeg
dried onion
dried oregano
onion powder
paprika
dried parsley
dry mustard (Colemans)
pepper
poppy seeds
poultry seasoning
dried rosemary
salt/Lite salt/salt substitute
sesame seeds
tabasco sauce
dried tarragon
dried thyme

Worcestershire Sauce
bacon soy bits
Molly McButter (natural butter)
Parsley Patch Salt Free Seasoning
taco seasoning
almond extract
maple extract
rum extract
vanilla extract
unbleached flour
whole wheat flour
cornstarch
cocoa
baking powder
baking soda
granulated sugar
Equal sweetener
brown sugar or
    brown sugar substitute
powdered sugar
honey (optional)
molasses
nonfat dry milk
cornflake crumbs
canola oil (Puritan or Canola
    West)
olive oil
non-stick cooking spray
Krusteaz Oat Bran Lite Pancake
    Mix
sugar-free instant vanilla pudding
    mix
sugar-free cherry Jello
sugar-free lime Jello

walnuts (optional)

**Canned Oriental Foods**
bean sprouts
chinese-style vegetables
water chestnuts
soy sauce (Kikkoman)
Marukan Seasoned Gourmet
    Rice Vinegar Lite Dressing
    or Marukan Rice Vinegar

**Canned Mexican Foods**
whole green chiles
diced green chiles
salsa, thick and chunky
enchilada sauce
vegetarian refried beans

**Canned and Packaged Fruits**
crushed pineapple (natural
    juice)
pineapple chunks (natural juice)
mandarin oranges
applesauce, unsweetened
lite cherry pie filling (Wilderness
    brand)
lemon juice
lime juice
raisins
dates

## Canned Vegetables and Legumes
*\* use "no salt added" if available*
artichoke hearts
tomato sauce\*
tomato paste
canned tomatoes\*
stewed tomatoes\*
tomato juice\*
sauerkraut
sliced/chopped mushrooms\*
pimento
green beans\*
whole kernel corn\*
creamed corn
vegetarian baked beans
garbanzo beans\*
kidney beans\*
black eyed peas\*
pinto beans\*
chilies (with beans):
    Cimmaron Chicken Chili
    Cimmaron Beef Chili
    Stagg Chicken Chili
    Nalley Chili Con Carne
    Fred Meyer Chili Con Carne

## Dressings, Sauces, Jams and Vinegar
reduced calorie mayonnaise (Best Foods Lite)
mustard mayonnaise (Mustard Farm-low fat)
Miracle Whip Lite
ranch style dressing mix (buttermilk type)
French's Au Jus Gravy Mix
low calorie French dressing
low calorie Italian dressing (Bernsteins)
chili sauce
seafood cocktail sauce
catsup
Dijon mustard
Roger Hong's Chinese Barbecue Sauce
Coleman's Hot English Mustard
S & W Mesquite Cooking Sauce & Marinade
Lea & Perrins White Wine Worcestershire Sauce
Kraft Sauceworks Sweet'n Sour Sauce
Old Spice Honey Mustard
Milani 1890 Dill Sauce
low sugar apricot jam
low sugar orange marmalade
vinegar
red wine vinegar
malt vinegar
Ragu Homestyle Spaghetti Sauce ( meatless)
Ragu 100% Natural Pizza Sauce

## Frozen Foods
chopped spinach
pea pods
peas
Oriental style vegetables (plain)
blueberries
strawberries
orange juice concentrate
Crystal Lite Popsicles
Egg Beaters (egg substitute)
bread dough

chicken breasts/ parts/turkey breast
ground beef (9% fat or less)
ground turkey (7% fat)
cooked, cubed chicken (diced)
cooked shrimp
fish fillets: cod, sole, snapper, halibut

## Produce
onions
chopped garlic
carrots
potatoes

## Pasta (eggless), Rice, and Dried Beans
elbow macaroni
angel hair pasta
fettucini noodles
lasagna noodles
spaghetti noodles
dried black eyed peas
pearl barley
dried green split peas
dried lentils
quick cooking brown rice

## Cereals, Crackers and Cookies
old fashioned or quick-cooking oatmeal
oat bran
Grapenuts
All Bran
Bran Buds or 100% Bran
whole grain cereals (less than 3 grams of fat per serving)

rice cakes
melba toast
RyKrisp (unseasoned)
unsalted top saltines
vanilla wafers
gingersnaps
graham crackers,
animal crackers
fig bars

### Soups and Soup Mixes
Swanson's beef broth
Swanson's chicken broth (30%
    less salt)
beef and chicken bouillon
    (regular or salt free)
tomato soup
chicken gumbo
dry vegetable soup mix

### Canned Seafood
water pack tuna
minced clams
red salmon

### Beverages
sugar-free hot cocoa mix
sugar-free soda pop:
    Fresca or Sprite
    cream, orange
sugar-free seltzer: raspberry
    (WinterBrook or New York)
apple juice
herbal teas
Crystal Light, lemon-lime

### Miscellaneous
peanut butter
pop corn
pretzels (available unsalted)
Parmesan cheese
dry sherry
dry white wine or vermouth

# GROCERY LIST: PERISHABLES

## Breads and Grains

(choose several)
whole wheat bread
English muffins
hamburger buns
Pita bread
French rolls
Focaccia bread
Boboli Italian bread shell
French bread
flour tortillas (6" size)
corn tortillas

## Dairy and Cheese

milk, skim or 1%
buttermilk
nonfat yogurt, plain
sweetened nonfat yogurt
   (Yoplait Light)
lite sour cream
low fat cottage cheese
low fat Ricotta cheese
feta cheese**
Light Philadelphia Cream
   Cheese Product (tub)
Laughing Cow Reduced Calorie
   Cheese Product
part-skim mozzarella cheese
Kraft Light Naturals (1/3 less fat)
   cheddar
margarine

## Fresh Vegetables

(choose enough for salad/raw
veggies and 2 for cooking)
cucumber
green onion
lettuce
radishes
tomatoes
mushrooms
celery
peppers: green, red, yellow
broccoli
cauliflower
zucchini
cabbage
spinach
asparagus

## Fresh Fruit

(choose 2-3 in season)
apples
oranges
grapefruit
strawberries
bananas
grapes
melons

## Meats, Poultry, and Seafood

top sirloin steak
round steak
rib pork chops
fresh oysters (jar)
imitation crab
sliced turkey Deli meats
Smoked Turkey Sausage (Louis
   Rich)
also see Frozen on "Staple List"

## Miscellaneous

Pillsbury's Best Sugar Cookie
   Dough**
angel food cake

** used in only one recipe

# WEEKLY GROCERY LIST

**Milk/Yogurt/Cheese/Eggs**

_____

_____

_____

**Canned & Packaged Foods**

_____

_____

_____

**Breads & Cereals**

_____

_____

_____

**Frozen Foods**

_____

_____

_____

**Fresh Vegetables**
(choose for salad or raw and 2 for cooking)

_____

_____

_____

**Fresh Fruit (2-3)**

_____

_____

_____

**Meat/Poultry/Seafood**

_____

_____

_____

**Sandwich/Lunch Makings**

_____

_____

_____

**Miscellaneous**

_____

_____

_____

_____

_____

_____

Choose an entreé for each main meal and check ingredients needed and add them to this list.

# GROCERY LIST: STAPLES

**Spices and Baking Products**
allspice
dried basil
bay leaves
celery seed
chili powder
dried cilantro
cinnamon
ground cloves
coriander
cumin
curry
dried dill
garlic powder
ginger
Italian herb seasoning
Kitchen Bouquet
liquid smoke
dried marjoram
nutmeg
dried onion
dried oregano
onion powder
paprika
dried parsley
dry mustard (Colemans)
pepper
poppy seeds
poultry seasoning
dried rosemary
salt/Lite salt/salt substitute
sesame seeds
tabasco sauce
dried tarragon
dried thyme

Worcestershire Sauce
bacon soy bits
Molly McButter (natural butter)
Parsley Patch Salt Free Seasoning
taco seasoning
almond extract
maple extract
rum extract
vanilla extract
unbleached flour
whole wheat flour
cornstarch
cocoa
baking powder
baking soda
granulated sugar
Equal sweetener
brown sugar or
    brown sugar substitute
powdered sugar
honey (optional)
molasses
nonfat dry milk
cornflake crumbs
canola oil (Puritan or Canola West)
olive oil
non-stick cooking spray
Krusteaz Oat Bran Lite Pancake Mix
sugar-free instant vanilla pudding mix
sugar-free cherry Jello
sugar-free lime Jello

walnuts (optional)

**Canned Oriental Foods**
bean sprouts
chinese-style vegetables
water chestnuts
soy sauce (Kikkoman)
Marukan Seasoned Gourmet Rice Vinegar Lite Dressing or Marukan Rice Vinegar

**Canned Mexican Foods**
whole green chiles
diced green chiles
salsa, thick and chunky
enchilada sauce
vegetarian refried beans

**Canned and Packaged Fruits**
crushed pineapple (natural juice)
pineapple chunks (natural juice)
mandarin oranges
applesauce, unsweetened
lite cherry pie filling (Wilderness brand)
lemon juice
lime juice
raisins
dates

## Canned Vegetables and Legumes

*  use "no salt added" if available
artichoke hearts
tomato sauce*
tomato paste
canned tomatoes*
stewed tomatoes*
tomato juice*
sauerkraut
sliced/chopped mushrooms*
pimento
green beans*
whole kernel corn*
creamed corn
vegetarian baked beans
garbanzo beans*
kidney beans*
black eyed peas*
pinto beans*
chilies (with beans):
    Cimmaron Chicken Chili
    Cimmaron Beef Chili
    Stagg Chicken Chili
    Nalley Chili Con Carne
    Fred Meyer Chili Con Carne

## Dressings, Sauces, Jams and Vinegar

reduced calorie mayonnaise
    (Best Foods Lite)
mustard mayonnaise (Mustard
    Farm-low fat)
Miracle Whip Lite
ranch style dressing mix
    (buttermilk type)
French's Au Jus Gravy Mix
low calorie French dressing

low calorie Italian dressing
    (Bernsteins)
chili sauce
seafood cocktail sauce
catsup
Dijon mustard
Roger Hong's Chinese Barbecue
    Sauce
Coleman's Hot English Mustard
S & W Mesquite Cooking Sauce
    & Marinade
Lea & Perrins White Wine
    Worcestershire Sauce
Kraft Sauceworks Sweet'n Sour
    Sauce
Old Spice Honey Mustard
Milani 1890 Dill Sauce
low sugar apricot jam
low sugar orange marmalade
vinegar
red wine vinegar
malt vinegar
Ragu Homestyle Spaghetti
    Sauce ( meatless)
Ragu 100% Natural Pizza
    Sauce

## Frozen Foods

chopped spinach
pea pods
peas
Oriental style vegetables (plain)
blueberries
strawberries
orange juice concentrate
Crystal Lite Popsicles
Egg Beaters (egg substitute)
bread dough

chicken breasts/ parts/turkey
    breast
ground beef (9% fat or less)
ground turkey (7% fat)
cooked, cubed chicken (diced)
cooked shrimp
fish fillets: cod, sole, snapper,
    halibut

## Produce

onions
chopped garlic
carrots
potatoes

## Pasta (eggless), Rice, and Dried Beans

elbow macaroni
angel hair pasta
fettucini noodles
lasagna noodles
spaghetti noodles
dried black eyed peas
pearl barley
dried green split peas
dried lentils
quick cooking brown rice

## Cereals, Crackers and Cookies

old fashioned or quick-cooking
    oatmeal
oat bran
Grapenuts
All Bran
Bran Buds or 100% Bran
whole grain cereals (less than 3
    grams of fat per serving)

rice cakes
melba toast
RyKrisp (unseasoned)
unsalted top saltines
vanilla wafers
gingersnaps
graham crackers,
animal crackers
fig bars

## Soups and Soup Mixes
Swanson's beef broth
Swanson's chicken broth (30%
    less salt)
beef and chicken bouillon
    (regular or salt free)
tomato soup
chicken gumbo
dry vegetable soup mix

## Canned Seafood
water pack tuna
minced clams
red salmon

## Beverages
sugar-free hot cocoa mix
sugar-free soda pop:
    Fresca or Sprite
    cream, orange
sugar-free seltzer: raspberry
    (WinterBrook or New York)
apple juice
herbal teas
Crystal Light, lemon-lime

## Miscellaneous
peanut butter
pop corn
pretzels (available unsalted)
Parmesan cheese
dry sherry
dry white wine or vermouth

# GROCERY LIST: PERISHABLES

## Breads and Grains
(choose several)
whole wheat bread
English muffins
hamburger buns
Pita bread
French rolls
Focaccia bread
Boboli Italian bread shell
French bread
flour tortillas (6" size)
corn tortillas

## Dairy and Cheese
milk, skim or 1%
buttermilk
nonfat yogurt, plain
sweetened nonfat yogurt
    (Yoplait Light)
lite sour cream
low fat cottage cheese
low fat Ricotta cheese
feta cheese**
Light Philadelphia Cream
    Cheese Product (tub)
Laughing Cow Reduced Calorie
    Cheese Product
part-skim mozzarella cheese
Kraft Light Naturals (1/3 less fat)
    cheddar
margarine

## Fresh Vegetables
(choose enough for salad/raw
veggies and 2 for cooking)
cucumber
green onion
lettuce
radishes
tomatoes
mushrooms
celery
peppers: green, red, yellow
broccoli
cauliflower
zucchini
cabbage
spinach
asparagus

## Fresh Fruit
(choose 2-3 in season)
apples
oranges
grapefruit
strawberries
bananas
grapes
melons

## Meats, Poultry, and Seafood
top sirloin steak
round steak
rib pork chops
fresh oysters (jar)
imitation crab
sliced turkey Deli meats
Smoked Turkey Sausage (Louis
    Rich)
also see Frozen on "Staple List"

## Miscellaneous
Pillsbury's Best Sugar Cookie
    Dough**
angel food cake

** used in only one recipe

**To order additional copies of Quick & Healthy, send check or money order to:**

Brenda Ponichtera, R.D.
1519 Hermits Way
The Dalles, Oregon 97058

– – – – – – – – – – – – – – – – – – – – – – – – – – – – –

## Quick & Healthy Cookbook Order Form

_____ copies at $16.95 per copy          $_____

Shipping & Handling ($2.00 per book)     $_____

                    Total Enclosed      $_____

Name_____

Address_____

City_____ State_____ Zip_____

– – – – – – – – – – – – – – – – – – – – – – – – – – – – –

## Quick & Healthy Cookbook Order Form

_____ copies at $16.95 per copy          $_____

Shipping & Handling ($2.00 per book)     $_____

                    Total Enclosed      $_____

Name_____

Address_____

City_____ State_____ Zip_____